Information Systems in Management

K. J. Radford

Department of Management Sciences
University of Waterloo, Waterloo,
Ontario, Canada

Reston Publishing Company, Inc., A Prentice-Hall Company
Reston, Virginia

©1973 by
RESTON PUBLISHING COMPANY, INC.
A Prentice Hall Company
Box 547
Reston, Virginia 22090

10   9   8   7   6   5   4   3   2

ISBN: 0-87909-352-8

Library of Congress Catalog Card Number: 73-80911
Printed in the United States of America.

Information Systems
in Management

Contents

Budgeting
Allocation of Resources to Activities
Establishing Measures of Effectiveness
The Program Budget
Budgeting for Support Activities
Managing of On-Going Operations
Other Aspects of Management

Rationality and Personalistic Involvement in Decision-Making
Completely Specified Decision Processes
Role of the Computer in Decision-Making

Methodology of Measurement
Data and Information
Aggregation of Data
Standards in Data Representation

The Administrative and Operational Systems
The Management Reporting System
The Common Data Base
The Information Retrieval System
The Data Management System
Operation of the System

The Existing Information System
Implementation–Phase I
Implementation–Phase II
Implementation–Phase III
Organization for Implementation
Operations

The Administrative and Operational Systems
Data Management
    The Data Management System
    Storage of Data
    Redundancy of Storage

Preface

Every organization, whether business, government, or industry has an information system. The role of this information system is to acquire, process, and communicate data that is essential to the operation of the organization. In most cases, the information system has developed naturally as the organization itself has developed. Its characteristics reflect the needs (past and present) of managers for information and communication in carrying out their day-to-day tasks.

There has recently been a growing awareness that an information system that has grown naturally over the years may not be the best to serve an organization in the changing environment in which it must operate today. For this reason, a number of organizations have made a specific effort to design and install an information system to meet the needs of their current and future management and decision-making tasks. The purpose of this book is to describe how the design and implementation of such an information system can be accomplished.

The first four chapters of the book are devoted to a review of management and decision making and of the nature of the data that the information system can process and present in support of these tasks. This is followed by a description of the components of an information system and of the detailed work of implementing such a system in a typical organization.

Preface

The best designed information system can succeed only if its implementation is supported by the members of the staff of the organization who need to use it. To many of these people, the need for such a system may not be immediately obvious. It is essential, therefore, that managers at all levels be involved in the design of an information system from the beginning and that information systems specialists and managers work together in the implementation. These conditions have not always been met in the past. A later chapter in the book deals with the impact of the implementation of a new system on an organization and suggests some methods for lessening the possibility of resistance to the development.

Costs and benefits of implementing an information system are dealt with in Chap. 9 along with means of evaluating the system during installation and after. The book ends with a detailed case history of all phases of design and implementation in a medium-size organization. The experience on which this case history is based was gathered in three major implementation projects. However, the details are presented in the context of one organization in order to present a cohesive description of the complete process of design and implementation.

During the preparation of this book, I have been most conscious of the help and encouragement of my colleagues in the Department of Management Sciences at the University of Waterloo. In particular, I am grateful to Professors Donald J. Clough and F. E. Burke who made many helpful suggestions on the early drafts. I am indebted also to Derek Jamieson of the University of Guelph for his assistance in many conversations during the period when the book was being planned; and to Pam Umbach who kept the many drafts in shape and prepared the final manuscript for the publisher.

My thanks are due also to the "Harvard Business Review" and to Professor John Dearden for permission to reproduce Figure 5-4 in Chap. 5; to the "Journal of Systems Management" for permission to use portions of an article which originally appeared in that journal in its June 1972 issue; and to Professors C. Argyris and S. Eilon and the Editors of "Management Science" for permission to reproduce excerpts of articles published in that journal.

K. J. Radford

1

Introduction

Information systems have existed in one form or another since the beginning of human enterprise. The importance of information in the management of an organization was recognized in ancient times. The histories of military campaigns and of governments provide a large number of examples of the establishment of systems to ensure the flow of information to decision makers.

As society and its accompanying technology have become more complex, the problems confronting managers in business, industry and government have become increasingly difficult. Compared with his counterpart of fifty years ago, the modern manager is faced with the need to make decisions in situations involving many more factors, with a far greater range of possible outcomes. The requirement in modern organizations for a system to provide information relating to these factors on a reliable and timely basis is a natural consequence of these developments.

1

The Growth of the Information System

As a point of departure in the study of information systems, let us consider a small enterprise in which the owner performs all or most of the tasks himself. In the context of a small country store, Sisson and Canning[1] and Murdick and Ross[2] have described how the proprietor fulfills for his own business all the functions undertaken in a modern organization by the comptroller, sales manager, public relations director, stores manager, chief of operations, etc. He gathers all the information needed to make decisions in each of these areas from actual and personal experience on the job and stores it in his memory. Data that are too numerous or too detailed to be retained in his memory are recorded in a ledger. The efficiency of the system is derived in part from the close relationship within the mind of the proprietor between the various functions that he performs and also from the fact that information required in these functions is recorded unequivocally in a single storage location (be it in the proprietor's memory or in the ledger, with which he is very familiar). Furthermore, information once stored can be applied, at will, to any of the functions that the proprietor undertakes. The maximum use is made of the information transmission and decision-making capabilities of the human system in conducting the business of the store.

This form of management and of the storage and use of information is ideal in the context of a small organization where the volumes of data are small, where the number of decisions required is small, and where the complexity of the decision-making processes is not high. It works well, also, in organizations where a small number of partners or employees work closely together. Over a period of time in such an organization, the high degree of commonality of experience and purpose provides an atmosphere in which close communication is maintained between the individuals and between their respective stores of information.

As the scope and complexity of business increases, the volume of data and the complexity of the decision-making processes involved increase in proportion. The expansion of product lines, the increased sales volume, and the greater scope of regulations governing the operations of companies have all combined to make the administration of a modern organization more complex. Greater numbers of employees are required to cope with this increased complexity and

[1]R. L. Sisson and R. G. Canning, *A Manager's Guide to Computer Processing,* Wiley, 1967.

[2]R. G. Murdick and J. E. Ross, *Information Systems for Modern Management,* Prentice Hall, 1971, pp. 155-158.

scope of business, and this in itself adds to the administrative workload. Employees must be paid; and modern society requires tax deductions at the source and systems for pension, unemployment and medical insurance, charitable donations, and union dues, all of which increase the volume of data to be processed on a regular basis. At the company level, corporation tax laws must be obeyed and sales tax collected and paid to the appropriate governments.

The effect of this increased complexity and volume of data is to place the tasks of data transmission, data storage, and decision making in most organizations outside the practical capability of one man or of a closely linked group of employees. This is not so much because the human brain is incapable of processing data in relation to the decision making tasks involved, but because the rate of data transmission to and from the decision and response centers in the human brain appears to be limited in practice.

Because of these characteristics of the human data acquisition and response systems, a single human being would be quickly and completely overcome by the amount of data generated and the number of responses required if he tried to manage a modern organization in the manner of the proprietor of an old-time country store. There are, to be sure, men who have controlled vast modern enterprises completely and directly from a central position, such as Mellon of U.S. Steel and K. C. Irving of New Brunswick; but these are exceptional men, with exceptional talents, using methods that have become less and less acceptable in our modern environment. The solution adopted by lesser men as their businesses have grown in volume and complexity has been to delegate portions of the work to partners and employees, thus lessening the volume of data and the number of decisions directly handled by themselves.

Delegation involves communication in both directions, to convey instructions and policies and to present reports on activities. The restricted rate of passage of information between individuals is of less concern in these communications if the context is fully known to both parties and if a wide area of experience is common to them (as between father and son in a family business, for example). Communication is less easy between employer and employees with less mutual experience, and recourse is therefore made to written instructions and reports which can be studied over a period of time. This reduces the necessary rate of acquisition of data. Written communications and reports are all the more necessary if the business expands to different geographic locations, thus lessening further the contacts between workers at the many levels in the organization. *However, the purpose of communication is defeated if the instructions are presented in such a way as to require acquisition and study of large amounts of data before reaching an understanding of the message.*

As business has become more complex, the tendency has been for employees in an organization to specialize in a particular function; for example, financial accounting, sales or personnel management. In most cases, each functional specialist has tended to keep his own data within his own component of the organization and in a form suited to his specialty. In large organizations, elements of data important to more than one function may be stored in two or more different locations, possibly in different forms, and sometimes without a common method of updating the data as time goes by. The integrated system used subconsciously by the proprietor of the country store has therefore been superseded by a number of semi-autonomous systems operating on a functional basis, and in some cases without overall coordination of the data and of the decision-making processes with which they are connected. The volume of data involved in modern organizations has often led to the need to introduce data handling machines and computers into these functional systems. This has typically been done on a system-by-system basis, without regard for the interdependence of the various functions in the running of the business. *The result of the introduction of computers has, in many cases, been to reduce the degree of standardization in the handling of data in the functional systems* and thereby to increase the autonomy of those systems within the organizations.

The method of operation of the modern organization is, therefore, a far cry from the compact and closely coupled handling of data and decision-making by the proprietor of the country store. The increased scope and complexity of modern affairs has taken the management of most organizations out of the realm of capability of a single human being. It has forced delegation of responsibility and thereby brought about the growth of a more formal written expression of instructions and reports to supplement the less formal interaction between members of the organization. Informal contacts between individuals have become less able to satisfy completely the need for communication because of the lessening of mutual experience among these members. The tendency towards specialization among staff members and the introduction of data processing machines and computers to handle the expanding volume of data have worked to lessen the interaction between components of the growing organization. The problem with which we are faced today is to examine communication between these components and to create an information system (incorporating both formal and informal aspects) designed to handle the growing amounts of data and to provide information to managers which is pertinent to their needs in decision making.

The Information System as a Component of an Organization

The importance of the information system as a necessary component of an organization was recognized by Norbert Wiener when he wrote:[3] ". . . the community extends only so far as there extends an effectual transmission of information." This remarkable pioneer in the science of cybernetics compared the processing and transmission of data by computers with the activities of the human nervous system.

It is interesting to note that perhaps the most complex organization existing today is the human body. In the simplest terms, the body consists of a metabolic system with the functions of ingesting resources (such as food and oxygen) and converting them to fuel required by the motor response systems (muscles) that undertake the actions that are necessary to the activities of the individual. The whole system is controlled by the brain, which monitors information transmitted to it on the internal functioning of the body, receives data on external stimuli detected by the senses, and makes decisions on the basis of criteria that are stored in the brain, much in the same way as a program is stored in a computer. The essential function of transmitting data to and from the components of the body is undertaken by the central nervous system. We shall see later than an information system designed to serve a modern complex organization resembles to some extent a combination of the central nervous system, part of the brain, and the sensors which detect and transmit data on internal and external stimuli.

The importance which Wiener attached to the information system as an integral part of an organization is shown by the following excerpt from his book entitled *Cybernetics:*[4]

> . . . any organism is held together . . . by the possession of a means for the acquisition, use, retention and transmission of information.

---

[3]Norbert Wiener, *Cybernetics,* The MIT Press, 1969, pp. 157-158.

[4]*Ibid.* p. 161.

In a more popular version of his original text on cybernetics, *The Human Use of Human Beings*,[5] he applied insights gained in computer technology to the study of human communications in society and in organizations in which human beings are essential components, and concluded that:

> ... society can only be understood through a study of the messages and the communications facilities that belong to it.

Wiener described a number of basic processes which are essential to an organism. For our purposes in studying an organization, these can be described under the headings: data capture and storage, communication, feedback and control, homeostasis, and entropy.

Data Capture and Storage

Just as the human system relies on the sensory organs and other sensitive mechanisms to capture data on internal and external circumstances, events and stimuli that affect its operation, an organization must rely upon sensing activities to capture data on the internal and external situations that confront it. These sensory activities take a number of different forms. Part of the data captured is collected by staff members in their normal activities, both within and outside the organization, in discussions, conferences, observations of events, and reading, for example. Certain other portions of the data captured may enter in the form of statistics and other information prepared by other agencies and possibly issued in a form readable only by data processing equipment. Yet another category arises from the filling out of forms, within the organization and in its contacts with outside agencies. Efficient operation of the organization depends in large part on the efficiency of these processes of data capture, not only in areas from which information has been useful in the past, but also on subjects and in areas that may well affect future activities. Furthermore, data once captured must be stored for future use in a manner that provides free and timely access without loss of information content.

Communication

The subject of communication within organizations has been dealt with by many authors, notably by Herbert A. Simon,[6] Pfiffner and

---

[5]Norbert Wiener, *The Human Use of Human Beings,* Avon Books, 1970, p. 25.

[6]Herbert A. Simon, *Administrative Behavior,* Free Press, 1965, pp. 154 et seq.

Sherwood,[7] and March and Simon.[8] Communication in organizations is a two-way process. As Simon points out,[6] it comprises both the transmittal of orders, information and advice to a decision center *and* the transmittal of the decisions reached from this center to other parts of the organization. The communication cannot be considered as complete in any one-way channel until the information transmitted has been received and understood in the context of the decision to which it refers. Similarly, in the second half of the two-way process, the communication is incomplete until data on the decisions reached and any necessary actions have been received and understood by the recipient.

Simon goes on to describe the relationship of the formal and informal channels of communication that were discussed earlier in this chapter in the context of the growth of the country store into a modern business. He lists the following media of formal communication: oral communications (in meetings, etc.), memoranda and letters, paper flow, records and reports and manuals, and points out the continuing need for flexibility in the form and content of these formal communications in keeping with the changing pattern of decision making in the organization.

No matter how elaborate a system of formal communication is set up in an organization, it will (and should) be complemented by an informal communications system. This informal system is much less structured than its formal counterpart and thereby achieves a much greater flexibility in changing conditions. On the other hand, it is less likely to cover all aspects of any situation confronting the organization. The informal communication system may be based to some extent on social relationships that exist in the organization. It may be used by some members of an organization to further their own (rather than the organization's) objectives. It is, nevertheless, a necessary complement to the more formal information system with which we are concerned in this book. By the same token, the establishment of a formal information system in an organization should not, in any way, be allowed to impede or restrict the informal system. The whole subject of communications in an organization is basic to the study of information systems and will be reopened in later chapters.

[6]Herbert A. Simon, *Administrative Behavior,* Free Press, 1965, pp. 154 et seq.

[7]J. M. Pfiffner and F. P. Sherwood, *Administrative Organization,* Prentice-Hall, 1960.

[8]J. G. March and Herbert A. Simon, *Organizations,* Wiley, 1958.

Feedback and Control

The concept of control by feedback is familiar to all who have observed the operation of a governor on a steam engine or of a thermostat in a home heating system. The essence of this concept is that information obtained by observation of current conditions is used to determine future behavior, within a given spectrum of possible future actions. Norbert Wiener compared control by feedback in living organisms and machines, observing that, ". . . they must be *en rapport* with the outer world by sense organs . . . which not only tell them what the existing circumstances are, but enable them to record the performance of their own tasks."[9] Pfiffner and Sherwood extended the analogy to include organizations,[10] saying that the give-and-take of goal-setting, communication, and continuous correction is not only the essence of feedback but also comprises the heart of coordination in large scale organizations. They go on to say that feedback may be more important in some types of enterprise than in others, but there is no organization in which it is not essential.[11]

The sensors designed to detect data on the internal and external situations that confront the organization are an essential component of the feedback and control process and therefore of the information system. As we have seen, data may reach the sensors in many forms. The sensors themselves may be of many different types, ranging from the manager himself, to groups and services specially employed to detect external data (such as, for example, market surveys), to automatic data readers and recorders engaged in data capture within the organization.

Homeostasis

Homeostasis is the property of striving toward equilibrium and stability in the face of internal and external changes and stimuli. It exists in living organisms and has been designed into many machines which are built to operate under automatic control. A number of observers have noted the existence of a similar phenomenon in organizations.[12] In ideal circumstances, the homeostatic process in

[9]Norbert Wiener, *The Human Use of Human Beings,* Avon Books, 1970, p. 47.

[10]J. M. Pfiffner and F. P. Sherwood, *Administrative Organization,* Prentice-Hall, 1960, p. 106.

[11]*Ibid.* p. 300.

[12]*Ibid.* p. 298.

an organization involves the maintaining of the activities of the organization within the bounds required to achieve specified goals and objectives and the modifying of these activities within this framework as a result of feedback from sensors detecting changes in internal and external conditions. Furthermore, although sometimes overlooked in organizations, it is essential in the homeostatic process that the data fed back be used to modify the goals and objectives and even the characteristics of the organization itself. This process is observed in living organisms, which adapt their way of life and, on occasion their physical structure, as a result of changes in their environment. The time scale on which they achieve this, however, is normally a great deal longer than that possible in the case of organizations. Homeostasis is not, therefore, a static process, but rather a means of ensuring stability in a dynamic environment. If the homeostatic process in an organization is allowed to become static (by default or by bad management) the organization is likely to become ineffective and may eventually die.

Entropy

The concept of entropy originated in thermodynamics where it is important as a measure of disorganization and disorder. The idea has been put forward[13] in the context of organizations that the increase of entropy can be resisted only by organization, and organization depends primarily on information. Organizational entropy and the entropies of statistical mechanics and information theory can be represented in similar mathematical terms. Thus, a useful relationship can be established between the two different entropies[14] using already developed mathematical methods. However, this is not regarded as a profitable approach at this stage in the study of information systems. Rather, it is suggested that organizations form local spaces in which the general increase of entropy is arrested and that the degree to which this takes place is determined by the purposefulness of the organization in striving towards its goals and objectives. This, in turn, is related to the amount of meaningful information flowing in the organization, where the word "meaningful" is taken as "usable in decisions concerning the activities undertaken by the organization in striving towards its goals and objectives."

Thus it is possible to imagine an organization in which the data

[13] *Ibid.* p. 297.

[14] J. R. Pierce, *Symbols, Signals and Noise,* Harper & Row, 1965, p. 24.

flow is very high, but where the data are not in a form which can be related to the necessary decisions. The result would be a high degree of disorder and a correspondingly small decrease in entropy by virtue of the organization. The same result would occur if the data were well related to the necessary decision processes, but were, in fact, ignored by the decision-makers. In order that the information system contribute to the purposefulness of an organization, the following two conditions must be satisfied.

1/ The data flowing must be *appropriate* to the necessary decision processes in the organization

2/ The data must be in a form that can be appreciated by the decision makers and the managers who direct activities as a result of the decisions. Furthermore, the data must be *used* in the decision making process.

The argument that data become information when they are put into a form that can be used in a decision-making process throws some light on the distinction between data and information. This reasoning will be developed in later chapters.

A First Approach to the Specification of an Information System

The foregoing discussion allows a first approach to the specification of an information system for an organization. In the broadest of terms:

- It must encompass formal and informal components.

- It must embrace sensors of all types necessary to capture data on internal and external conditions related to situations that confront the organization (or may confront it in the future).

- It must provide communication channels from the sensors to the decision making centers (people, groups of people and machines controlled by people).

- It must include storage facilities for data not immediately required or that may be required to be used more than once.

- It must have facilities for aggregating and collating data in order to convert them into information bearing on the decision processes necessary to the organization.

- It must provide channels of communication from the decision centers to the persons responsible for carrying out the necessary activities.

- It must provide output information in a readily comprehensible form to those persons and machines involved in the activities of the organization.

The method of creating an information system of this nature in an organization is the subject of the remaining chapters of this book. Because the information system must serve management in its quantitative aspects and in decision making, these matters are dealt with first. This leads to a review of the measurements, data and information that are necessary to the management of an organization.

Having established the requirements the information system must meet, a logical diagram can be derived showing the linkages between the essential components of the system which acquire, process and retain management information. This diagram can act as an overall guide in the implementation of an information system. However, in approaching such an implementation, it is important to recognize that an information system of one type or another already exists in all organizations. A first step must be to examine this existing system in detail in order to determine its efficiency and effectiveness for the purposes of the organization which it serves. The process of implementation then becomes that of moving from the existing system to one based on the managerial and decision making requirements of the organization.

A major component of all organizations consists of individual people, most of whom are dedicated to their work and perform in the best way they know how, considering the constraints under which they are working. To many of these people, a new information system is not the boon of which the specialist implementing it confidently speaks. To some the development may appear as a threat. The best designed information system is of little use if it is not embraced and used by the people in the organization. For this reason, the human factors encountered in the implementation of an information system are discussed in one of the later chapters of the book.

A complete case history of the first four years of implementation of a management information system designed according to the principles described is given in Chapter 10.

Discussion Topics

1/ What factors contribute most to the need for a formal information system as an organization grows? How do factors external to the organization affect the requirements for an information system?

2/ How does the *formal* component of the information system relate to the *informal* component? Is this relationship likely to be constant over time and changing circumstances?

3/ What factors can lead to a reduction of the degree of standardization of data in organizations? How can this reduction be minimized?

4/ Is there a conceptual connection between an organism (as discussed by Wiener) and an organization in modern society? What conclusions relating to information systems in modern organizations can be drawn from Wiener's work relating to organisms?

5/ What is the relationship between *feedback* and *control* in an organization and *homeostasis*? Is homeostasis a process that inhibits change? Give examples of homeostasis in organizations with which you are familiar.

6/ Is the concept of entropy useful in studying organizations? How could the degree of "disorganization" of an organization be measured, and how could that measure be related to the effective use of information?

7/ Is the analogy between an information system and the central nervous system in the human body useful in defining the desirable characteristics of the information system in an organization?

8/ What form might the "sensors" referred to by Wiener take in an organization?

2

Quantitative Aspects of Management

In the simplest terms, *an organization is an entity created to fulfill a purpose.* This purpose is concerned with the creation of *outputs.* The *inputs* to the organization are resources, which can be thought of in terms of raw materials, space and facilities and the efforts of human beings and machines. It is these inputs that are used in the creation of outputs. The purpose of the organization can therefore be simply stated as the conversion of input resources to outputs.

There may be an immediate objection to this simple view of the purpose of an organization if output is thought of solely in terms of goods from a production line. Many organizations do not produce goods in any form, but nevertheless have products. For example, a broadcasting company produces programs which have characteristics and qualities of far greater scope than the reels of video tape on which they are recorded. A school or university produces learning experiences for the participants in its activities. Governments provide services to the population.

13

Organizations may therefore be thought of as purposeful systems[1] which strive to meet objectives in terms of outputs which the organization was created to provide. The degree to which the objectives are met is a measure of the purposefulness of the organization. The role of management is to maximize this purposefulness in the face of the constraints imposed by internal and external conditions.

Goals and Objectives

It follows from the above discussion that an organization must have objectives. These must be related to the *function* of the organization as expressed, for example, in its terms of reference or its charter under the law. Furthermore, the objectives of an organization, or the area of application of these objectives, may alter with time and changing conditions. It is a major function of management to ensure that the objectives of the organization are continually reviewed in order that it may be kept purposeful as conditions change. For example, the objectives of the Emergency Measures Organization, which was set up initially to protect the population from the after-effects of a nuclear attack, have now been modified to give greater emphasis to protection against the effects of natural catastrophes. If objectives are not kept continually under review, the organization may become less purposeful and less appropriate under changed conditions. This may ultimately result in it being disbanded, although one usual, and sometimes unstated, objective of an organization is to ensure its own survival.

The objectives of an organization can seldom be described in a single, simply stated goal, although this may appear to be the case in a first approach to some organizations. It is assumed in many businesses, for example, that the sole objective is to maximize the return on investment. Even if this were the case, as has been pointed out by Christenson,[2] does this mean maximization in the short term, or in the long term, and how are these terms defined? Even if maximization of return on investment were the major objective (and even though the terms in which this return is to be obtained were defined), a number of contributing, or sub-objectives, might need to be stated. These sub-objectives are usually necessary to the achieve-

[1]Russell L. Ackoff and Fred E. Emery, *On Purposeful Systems,* Aldine-Atherton, 1972.

[2]Charles Christenson, "Some Lessons in Business from PPBS"; included in *Analysis for Planning Programming Budgeting,* Washington Operations Research Council, Washington, D.C. 1968, p. 59.

ment of the main objective, but may in fact conflict with it in the short or long term. For example, a sub-objective of maintaining the public image of the company may well detract from short-term profits but be essential to the maintenance of return on investment in the long term. Substantial sums being spent on the reduction of pollution from manufacturing plants, and on informing the public of this investment, provide a present-day example of this phenomenon.

Most organizations have multiple objectives. Some members of the set of objectives may have more importance than others at any one time, but nonetheless all objectives which are necessary to the purpose of the organization must be taken into account by management. It is common to think that business organizations are more single-minded than those in the public sector and are therefore less likely to be concerned with a multiplicity of objectives. This may be true of smaller business organizations; but the larger a business organization becomes, the more diverse its interests tend to be, and the more likely it is to have multiple objectives.

Individual objectives in a multiple set may or may not be independent of all the other members of the set. In some cases, two or more objectives may be in conflict. For example, a television station may desire to attract large audiences but may be required by a regulatory body to broadcast public affairs programs which are known to attract smaller audiences than entertainment programs. In this case, the station may be said to have objectives of attracting large audiences and of meeting the required proportion of public affairs offerings. The second objective may, however, be thought of as a constraint on achievement of the first. In this sense, all objectives in a multiple set may act as constraints on the others. This is particularly the case when resources are limited and allocation of some amount of resources towards the achievement of one objective reduces the amount of resources which can be used towards the achievement of the others.

More generally, when the members of a set of multiple objectives are not all independent of each other, or when resources are limited, conflict may arise. The result of this conflict will be that the pursuit of one objective to the point of optimum achievement will cause a lower degree of achievement toward the other objectives of the set. A further role of management is, therefore, to decide the degree to which individual objectives of a set are to be pursued, taking into account conflicts that may arise and the action of certain objectives as constraints on the achievement of the others.

This process is called *conditional* or *sub-optimization*.[3] Unless it is carefully practiced, one objective may be pursued at the expense of the others and to the overall detriment of the organization. For example, at a recent conference on military operational research, a Dr. X gave a paper concerning the mathematical derivation of an optimum pattern of depth charges fired from a destroyer. After he had finished, a Naval officer in the audience said, "But Dr. X, if you use that particular pattern, you will blow the stern off the destroyer." Dr. X replied, "That may be so, but that wasn't my problem. I was concerned only with deriving the optimum pattern of depth charges that should be laid."

Formulation of Objectives

A statement of objectives is the foundation of the whole work of an organization and should therefore be formulated with care. As a general guide, the objectives should be:

- Well thought out and explicitly stated.

- Directly related to the function of the organization.

- Stated in a form easily communicable to members of the organization.

- Defined so that methods of measuring performance in achieving the objectives can be readily devised.

- Defined with sufficient precision that the activities supporting one objective can be identified from those supporting another.

- Stated so as to permit and encourage the postulation of alternative methods of achieving the objectives.

It is important that the objectives should not be so general as to be almost meaningless when the time comes to relate programs of activity to them. For example, the objective of "fostering the well-being of the population" is a good-sounding objective, sometimes put forward by governments. However, without specification of the areas in which this should be done, it is almost impossible to translate into action.

Statements of objectives prepared for organizations sometimes contain only those items that management is prepared to see

[3]Charles J. Hitch, "Suboptimization in Operations Problems," Journal of the Operations Research Society of America, Vol. 1, No. 3, May 1953, pp. 87-99.

published. It is very natural that a business organization should not wish to reveal objectives that might alert a possible competitor to future activities. Under these circumstances, statements are published consisting of what may be termed *overt* objectives, while there remains in company confidential files, a supplementary list of *covert* objectives. In some cases, the overt and covert objectives may be mildly contradictory and even in direct conflict. Both sets are important in the creation of an information system, since management policies and decision-making are necessarily related to *all* objectives of the organization. An information system that relates to only the overt objectives will serve only a portion of the management activity. Similarly, if only covert objectives are taken into account in the design, the information system will not cover all the activities in the organization. Specification and listing of covert objectives may touch upon the most confidential matters in the organization, but they are nonetheless necessary as a preliminary to information system design.

Objectives of Components of an Organization

The foregoing discussion has referred entirely to the objectives of the organization as a whole. Alongside these objectives, each sub-group in the organization, from a major division down to the individual staff member, has objectives that may be explicitly stated or which may exist in implicit form. Ideally, the objectives of each component of an organization should be a sub-set of those of the whole. In practice, however, this is not always the case.

In the early stages of the life of an organization, the sense of purpose is usually strong. Direction of the enterprise is in the hands of a small group of men who work together singlemindedly and who delegate tasks to subordinates who are similarly inspired by the initial objectives of the organization. The personal objectives of staff members are closely linked to those of the organization by the feeling that success will bring high personal rewards. Intelligent management seeks to maintain this situation in the face of the diffusing effects of growth of the organization, frustration by external conditions, and conflicts between personalities. However, frequently the tendency is for the objectives of components, and of individuals, to diverge from those of the organization, so that the organization disintegrates slowly and falls short of the standards of effectiveness and competence that are set in the early days. This phenomenon has been called *organizational entropy.*[4] The decrease of effectiveness is related to the decrease in purposefulness and to an increase in the disorder existing in the management of the organization. The counter to this tendency lies in a continued and meaningful review of objectives, both of the organization as a whole and of the component parts. A concurrent evaluation of progress achieved towards those objectives is also necessary.

Objectives have an important relationship to the homeostatic processes in the organization and in its component parts. They are the premises on which management and control of an organization are based. As such, they are the starting point from which the specifications of the management process are derived, either implicitly or explicitly.

In the foregoing discussion, the word *objectives* could equally well have been replaced by *goals.* It is convenient convention, however, that will be followed hereafter, to use the word *objectives* when long term purposes are described and without relation to a particular time period. *Goals* can then be used to refer to progress that is planned or expected in a fixed time such as a fiscal year, or any other planning, period in the life of the organization.

Planning and Budgeting

Planning is concerned with finding the best ways of using resources in achieving the goals and objectives of an organization. The result of planning should be the choice of *tasks* or *activities* that will contribute most to the achievement of objectives. This is followed by the allocation of available resources to these activities in a manner related to the expected achievements in each.

The establishment and continual review of objectives is, therefore, an essential preliminary to planning. In dealing with the whole organization, the first step in planning is to define *program categories* which are ". . . groupings of agency programs (or activities or operations) which serve the same broad objective (or mission) or which have generally similar objectives."[5] This may seem to imply that all program categories should be mutually independent. In

[4]Chris Argyris, *Intervention Theory and Method,* Addison Wesley, 1970, pp. 56-88.

[5]U.S. Bureau of the Budget, Bulletin 66-3, October 12, 1965, Section 5.

practice this is not usually possible or even desirable. As Charles Christenson says[6] :

> For example, a program category such as "increasing knowledge about health problems" might very well include some contract research activities which have the incidental benefit of improving higher education, even though that is not their primary objective. A program structure which is too disaggregated will lead to a great many such cross effects and consequent analytical difficulties in comparing alternative programs, while one which is too highly aggregated leads us back in the direction of "maximizing welfare" and its attendant problems.

Program categories are the highest level in the hierarchy that comprises the activities of an organization. If necessary, program sub-categories can be defined as an intermediate step between this highest level and the *program elements.* Program elements have been defined as follows[7] :

> A program element covers agency activities related directly to the production of a discrete agency output, or group of related outputs. Agency activities which contribute directly to the output should be included in the program element, even though they may be conducted within different organizations, or financed from different appropriations. Thus, program elements are the basic units of the program structure.
> Program elements have these characteristics:

1/ They should produce clearly-definable outputs, which are quantified wherever possible.

2/ Wherever feasible, the output of a program element should be an agency end product, not an intermediate product that supports another element.

3/ The inputs of an element should vary with changes in the level of the output, but not necessarily proportionately.

---

[6]Charles Christenson, "Program Budgeting," Study supported under contract PH 108-67-10S "Quantitative Analysis in Health Services Administration," Graduate School of Business Administration, Harvard University, p. 13.

[7]U.S. Bureau of the Budget, Bulletin 68-9, April 12, 1968.

The Program Structure

The process just described leads to a *program structure* for the organization consisting of:

1/ Program categories.

2/ Program sub-categories.

3/ Program elements.

4/ Program sub-elements.

This structure should include all the activities being undertaken by the organization. It does not, however, necessarily include all the activities that *should* be undertaken. One of the essential tasks of planning at any level in an organization is the search for activities that will contribute to the achievement of objectives, but which have not yet been assessed or tried in this particular organization. Part of the planning function is a systematic analysis of all activities in support of achievement of a particular objective in order to determine which of the activities are likely to contribute most to the desired outputs per unit of input resource.

It is not unusual that the process of establishing a program structure in an existing organization reveals activities that at first glance have no relation to the objectives of the organization that have been formulated as the first step in the process. If this occurs, it is a good reason for review of the statement of objectives to determine whether something has been missed or omitted. On the other hand, the activities that are discovered may relate to objectives of a component of the organization, a group of persons, or an individual, which are in conflict with those of the organization as a whole. The discovery can therefore be the start of a process of rationalization, the end product of which may be the inclusion of the objectives of the component in those of the organization as a whole or, at the other end of the scale, the cancellation of the activities altogether. This phenomenon is noticed frequently in organizations where management has neglected the setting of comprehensive and meaningful objectives and goals over a long time period. In these circumstances, staff entering the organization and not receiving the necessary direction, often turn to activities that interest them and which they can perform well. The fact that these activities consume resources may well be to the detriment of the organization. On the other hand, these activities may contribute achievements toward objectives which should, in fact, be included in those of the organization.[8]

An example of a program structure is given in Table 10-2 as part of the case history description in Chapter 10.

Relationship of the Program Structure to the Organization Chart.

The program structure should be established independently of any established organization chart, which may unduly reflect past decisions and conflicts within the organization. The recommended approach is to allocate responsibility for activities after the objectives and program structure have been defined in an atmosphere free of organizational considerations. This ideal allocation of responsibility may, however, be very difficult to implement in practice, especially in a mature organization. Changes in the organization chart may be resisted by personnel because of a perceived threat to status and security and may therefore need to be implemented slowly and with considerable care. It is altogether possible to have two or more program elements under one organizational unit, or, alternatively, two or more organizational units contributing to the same program element. It is undesirable, of course, to have two or more organizational units responsible for the same activity. The ideal situation which can be worked toward occurs when the organization chart and the program structure can be completely related, with no duplication of activity or responsibility, no activity lacking a responsible organizational unit, and no unit without responsibility for an activity or activities in the program structure. In practice, however, the greater inertia associated with the organization chart, especially in large and mature organizations, may cause this aspect to lag behind the program structure. This effect is more pronounced if it is necessary to change the program structure often in response to changes in the external environment in which the organization works.

Budgeting

The need for budgeting rests on two basic facts. Firstly, resources are usually limited (if resources are unlimited, budgeting is unnecessary). Secondly, it is generally required to make the best possible use of the resources available.

Christenson has outlined the development of budgeting in four

---

[8]K. J. Radford, "Some Observations on the Analogy between Management Science and Medicine" INFOR Volume 9, No. 3, November 1971, pp. 238-247.

steps.[9] The first is a method of cash balance control by organizational sub-unit, in which the cash remaining in an allocation to a unit is monitored. If the cash balance appears to be getting too low in relation to the time remaining in the period for which the allocation is made, expenditures are cut back. This is similar to the way many people manage their personal finances. It is probably sufficient for very simple activities where the objective is well understood.

As organizations and their activities become more complex, a second factor is needed to allow management to determine not only how much has been spent, but also the areas, such as personnel, materials, supplies, equipment, etc., in which the expenditures have been made. Budgets are prepared therefore not only by organizational sub-unit, but also by *object of expenditure.* This type of budgeting persists today in many organizations.

A third dimension has been added in recent times based on the need to know *how* money was being used. The first Hoover Commission in the USA urged in 1949 that a budget ". . . based upon functions, activities and projects . . ." be prepared. Christenson points out that once the activities of an organizational sub-unit have been defined, it becomes possible to develop appropriate measures of the performance of these sub-units. This approach is called *performance budgeting,* and it has been widely used to evaluate the efficiency of sub-units in terms of their performance relative to the amounts allocated in the budget.

The final development results in a *program budget.* In this budget, amounts are allocated to an organizational sub-unit in terms of the parts of the program structure for which they are responsible. A program budget can be used to evaluate the *effectiveness* of an organizational sub-unit, and of the program to which it contributes, in achieving the objectives of the organization. As the final stage in the development to date, program budgeting encompasses the three earlier methods, all of which have a place in the management of the organization. The program budget is, however, the only one of the four types of budgets described which can be considered as an instrument of policy in the organization and which relates to its overall effectiveness with regard to its objectives. By comparison, the performance budget is useful primarily in monitoring the *efficiency* of the organization or of its components. A budget by object of expenditure has a role in the control of expenditures and a cash

[9]Charles Christenson, "Program Budgeting," Study supported under contract PH 108-67-10S "Quantitative Analysis in Health Services Administration," Graduate School of Business Administration, Harvard University, pp. 6-9.

balance budget is necessary to monitor cash flow.

The difference between *efficiency* and *effectiveness* as defined above can be illustrated by a simple example. Consider a factory manufacturing the pesticide DDT a few years ago. Its objective, in simple terms, was to maximize return on investment, and its efficiency was measured in terms of its performance in converting input resources to DDT. Under these circumstances, its effectiveness in meeting its objective was closely related to its efficiency. When the ban on the casual use of DDT was imposed, this did not alter the efficiency of the factory; but it had a profound effect on the effectiveness of the factory in meeting its objective, because the market for the product was substantially reduced. In effect, the factory had to search for a new and more appropriate activity in order to restore its effectiveness in striving toward its objective. In the simple case described this would almost certainly have been clear to management, whether they were working on a system of performance budgeting or on a program budget. In a more complex organization with multiple objectives and many activities, however, more time might have elapsed before management made an adjustment.

The program budget is therefore directly related to objectives and to the program structure established as a first step in achieving these objectives. It establishes all the resources required by the program elements and explicitly considers the resource requirements of activities over their lifetimes, which may extend into future budgetary periods. The program budget is organized by identifiable program elements rather than by objects of expenditure, although control budgets in terms of these objects may be related to it. The allocations of resources in the program budget are directly linked to the outputs of the organization necessary to achieve objectives. The question arises now of how these allocations are made between program elements when resources are limited and when program elements may contribute in different degrees to the achievement of objectives.

Allocation of Resources to Activities

The ideal method of allocation of resources to activities would be to measure the contribution of each activity to the achievement of objectives, determine the individual contributions per unit of resources expended in past experience, and then allocate resources in future budgets in such a way as to maximize expected achievement. This ideal is seldom feasible for a number of reasons. Firstly, it is extremely difficult to measure exactly the contribution of an activity toward an objective, except in the most simple of situations. Objectives are seldom such that it is possible to assess achievement in terms of a single quantitative parameter. Even if these were the case, it would not be correct, necessarily, to assume that a simple relationship existed between the application of resources and the degree of progress toward the objective. In most practical situations in modern affairs, the degree of achievement of objectives is far too complex to be described by a simple analytical model.

Nevertheless, the fact remains, that when management agrees upon a budget, an allocation of resources between activities has been made which *implies* a judgment of the expected achievements of these activities toward the objectives of the organization. For example, a city council may allocate resources to several life-saving activities, such as fire and rescue services, ambulance service, and provision of barriers at grade crossings. An increase in allocation to any one activity will result in more saving of life; and, distasteful as it may be, a dollar figure needed to save an extra life can no doubt be calculated for each activity. This approach is sometimes attacked on the grounds that human life is beyond price. Nevertheless, the city council in making any specific budget allocations to these services *implicitly* places a value on human life. Is it not better to study these matters explicitly?

Managerial intuition diligently applied has an uncanny quality of providing near optimum solutions to the problem of resource allocation; but there are sufficient cases of failure in this respect and of inability to determine whether the allocation was near-optimum or not to encourage us to explore methods of applying quantitative analysis to the resources allocation problem. This must not be done with the aim of replacing managerial intuition and judgment but rather to devise aids to management in carrying out this difficult role.

Establishing Measures of Effectiveness

The search for a more quantitative method of allocating resources to activities requires, as a first step, an attempt to establish measures of effectiveness in achieving objectives. In cases where the objective can be simply stated, such as "maximizing the average return on investment over the next five years," this is not difficult. With relatively little effort, a quantitative measure can be associated with the phrase "average return on investment"; and as long as the definition of this measure is not equivocal, it will serve to evaluate the contribution of each activity to the achievement of the objective.

In most cases in practice, the task is not as simple; and quantitative measures of achievement of objectives are not as easy to define. However, ". . . it is important to determine first what we should want to measure without being restricted by our current ability to measure things—we should avoid prejudging, based on current practice, what may be measurable and what may not be."[10]

The measures that must be sought are measures of output related to objectives; that is to say, true measures of effectiveness. Measures of efficiency, such as "number of units manufactured" or "number of units inspected" are not appropriate in this context, although they may well have a place in assessments of the efficiency of processes. Very few activities can be assessed in terms of a single objective, so that more than one measure of effectiveness may apply to any one activity. In such cases, there is a temptation to translate each measure into a common index, such as dollars saved, or to use weighting factors to combine measures that are expressed in different units into a single overall index of worth. If this is overdone, worthwhile information contained in the individual measures may be lost by virtue of an arbitrary choice of weighting factors. The result is to risk rejection of the whole scheme of measurement which has probably been carefully and painstakingly constructed by the addition of a final step based on arbitrary choice of weights. The quest for a set of effectiveness measures should go only so far, at any given time, as reasoned logic will allow. If the manager wishes later to go further in assessing weights in his process of decision-making, this is his right and his responsibility.

In some cases, where the establishment of direct measures has proved too difficult in the time available for the task, it may be necessary to resort to proxy measures. Hatry gives the example of measurement of ambulance response times in a study of an emergency service system.[11] In this case, it is assumed that quicker response is directly related to benefit to the patient; but before this proxy measure could be extensively used, a study of this relationship would undoubtedly be necessary.

The choice of a measure of effectiveness can itself influence the results of an evaluation of activities. Gross studied the allocation of

[10]Harry P. Hatry, "Measuring the Effectiveness of Non-Defense Public Programs," Journal of the Operations Research Society of America, Vol. 18, No. 5, Sept./Oct. 1970, p. 772-784.

[11]*Ibid*, pp. 779-780.

funds to costs of government health programs.[12] On the basis of "the number of deaths averted," a program against uterine cervical cancer showed high benefits. When the criterion was changed, however, to "saving of productive earnings of the people involved," a program against arthritis, a crippling, more than a killing disease, was seen as worthwhile.

Considerable care should be exercised in the choice of proxy measures. The relationship between the proxy and the objective to which it refers should be investigated thoroughly and explained to decision-makers on the presentation of results. More will be said on the subject of measurement in Chapter 4 and examples of the choice of measures are given in the case history described in Chapter 10.

The Program Budget

From the foregoing discussion, the main elements of the process of preparing the program budget can be seen as:

1/ A clear and explicit statement of the objectives of the organization.

2/ A listing and brief description of alternative activities which may satisfy these objectives.

3/ A program structure, consisting of groupings of program elements, or activities, each of which groupings constitute a feasible method of satisfying the objectives.

4/ An analysis of proposed alternatives serving to clarify objectives and evaluate the proposals against these objectives.

5/ A proposed schedule for implementing the preferred group of alternatives.

The end results of this process are:

1/ The program budget, a multi-year document which lists the preferred programs and the major activities of the organization, identifies costs associated with each program and provides estimates of benefits expected. This enables the decision maker to see the future implications of today's choices and evaluate the organization's progress toward its objectives.

[12]Robert N. Grosse, "Cost Benefit Analysis and Social Planning" in *Analysis for Planning Programming Budgeting* Washington Operations Research Council, Washington, D.C., 1968, pp. 135-138.

2/ A budget formally linked to planning. This tie ensures that budgets are derived from the purposes and objectives of the organization and not vice versa.

3/ An analytical process which underpins the whole by investigating proposed alternatives and placing before the decision-maker the relevant data organized in a way most useful to him.

4/ A budget that can be revised as conditions and objectives change, rather than only on a fixed budgetary cycle.

Budgeting for Support Activities

There are certain activities that are necessary to the operation of an organization, but do not result directly in an output related to an objective. These may be described as common or support activities. The office of the president or head of the organization is one example; common services that have been centralized for reasons of efficiency (for example, pension fund administration) provide others. The question arises whether the budgets and costs of these activities should be distributed among the program elements that they support or whether they should be the subject of a separate allocation of funds.

It is generally agreed by practitioners that arbitrary allocations made for the sole purpose of distributing costs should be avoided but that allocations that contribute to better decisions should be encouraged.[7] When supervisory and support services are completely involved in a single program element, the budgets and costs should be reflected in that element. If these services support two or more program elements, the budgets and costs should be distributed between these elements, provided that there is a reasonable basis for doing so. Otherwise, a separate classification should be included in the program structure to reflect these activities.

Since support activities of this nature are not directly related to output towards the achievement of an objective, it is not usually possible to assess them in terms of measures of effectiveness, as is the case with output-oriented activities. However, the efficiency of provision of these services can be considered in terms of *performance* measures, as discussed earlier. The cost per mile of transportation provided by a car pool or the administration costs per million dollars invested in a pension fund are examples of such performance measures. Some of the more adventurous amongst us might consider

[7] U.S. Bureau of the Budget, Bulletin 68-9, April 12, 1968.

the question of a suitable measure for the office of the head of the organization.

Management of On-going Operations

It is said that General Montgomery went to bed on the eve of the Battle of Alamein and gave orders that he should not be disturbed, even though the battle was due to start that night. By doing so, he wished to indicate confidence in his planning and allocation of resources and also to ensure that he would be refreshed when he was needed to make decisions as a result of reports from the front.

The manager who has spent considerable time on planning and budgeting might take the same point of view. As long as his operations are proceeding according to plan, he need not be concerned, apart from monitoring the expenditure of resources and progress toward achieving objectives. His work of decision-making will come into play only when the results reported deviate from the plan and when these results and the messages he receives about the environment in which he is operating indicate that a change of objectives or a change of plan, or both, is required.

Of course, this is a much over-simplified view of management. It refers only to the quantitative aspects and does not include major work areas such as personnel management, public relations and communication, which may occupy the majority of a manager's time. It does point out, however, the requirement for the information system to provide timely and periodic reports on progress toward objectives and use of resources compared with budget estimates for the time period in question. The frequency at which these reports are required is dependent on the activities in question and also upon the manager's preferences in receiving information. Also, many managers prefer to receive only reports on deviations from the budgeted figures and to operate under a system that has been called *management by exception.*[13]

To supplement reports relating progress to use of resources, the manager needs a system of control of expenditure of resources, which may be termed *responsibility accounting.*[14] This is a ". . . system designed to control expenditures by directly relating the reporting of expenditures to the individuals in the company

[13]J. M. Pfiffner and F. P. Sherwood, *Administrative Organization,* Prentice-Hall, 1960, p. 137.

[14]John A. Higgins, "Responsibility Accounting," The Arthur Anderson Chronicle, Vol. 12, No. 2, April 1952.

organization who are responsible for their control." The information reported by this system may be organized by object of expenditure (as in performance budgeting) or in any other way helpful to management in performing its tasks. "It is a system that emphasizes information that is useful to the operating management and deemphasizes the accounting and bookkeeping aspects that clutter up so many of our accounting and financial statements today."[14]

The reports of progress in program elements by use of resources and reports of expenditures by standard objects are closely related and have much data in common. These reports form that part of the information system called the "management reporting system" in this treatment. Details of the structure of the management reporting system and of the method of implementing this system are contained in the following chapters.

The reports contained in the management reporting system provide managers with a basis for evaluation of achievements compared with those planned and for monitoring the use of resources compared with the planned allocations. As a result of this evaluation, plans and allocations of resources may be changed during the fiscal period to which the plan refers. This method of directing on-going operations is similar to that which has been termed *management by objectives.*[15] This is described as a system under which the goals of the organization are identified and responsibilities distributed among individual managers in such a way that their combined efforts are directed towards achieving those goals.[16] The original thrust of this system was toward a method of allowing managers to plan and evaluate their own performance and that of their subordinates. An information system designed to assist in monitoring the performance of the whole organization and of its components can clearly be extended to serve this additional purpose.

A longer term aspect of evaluation concerns the assessment of achievements in program elements in conjunction with the planning and budgeting process for the next time period. Information on past achievements and expenditures of resources is an important input to the systematic analysis of activities proposed for the future. It is necessary, therefore, that data appearing in management reports be stored for later retrieval and use in these analyses. These data form a

[14]John A. Higgins, "Responsibility Accounting," The Arthur Anderson Chronicle, Vol. 12, No. 2, April 1952.

[15]Peter F. Drucker, *The Practice of Management,* Harper & Row, 1954.

[16]George S. Odiorne, *Management by Objectives,* Pitman, 1965, pp. 54-67.

body of historic information which supports the planning function and which can be recovered, together with its context, as the occasion demands. It is essential therefore that the information system provide facilities for the retention of these data for as long as they are pertinent to the operations of the organization.

Other Aspects of Management

The classic definition of the elements of management can be attributed to Henri Fayol.[17] Fayol concluded that management comprised five elements: planning, organizing, commanding, coordinating and controlling. These elements have been condensed into three in the foregoing discussion: planning and budgeting, directing of on-going operations and evaluation.

Since the publication of Fayol's original papers in the French language in 1916 and the publication by Frederick W. Taylor of his *Principles of Scientific Management* in 1911,[18] a considerable number of works dealing with management and organization theory has appeared. These works are summarized briefly in many modern publications,[19,20] and this need not be repeated here. The development starts from the scientific principles of Taylor, in which tasks undertaken are planned on the assumption that workers act as largely unthinking components of the organization and are motivated primarily by money. These ideas were modified considerably by the results of the Hawthorne experiments which showed productivity was affected in the late 1920's and 1930's, to a great extent by human factors. These experiments led to greater concern for human relations, especially in the areas of production.

The rapid growth of operations research and mathematical modeling during World War II provided techniques of quantitative analysis that were applied to business as soon as the war ended. At the same time, there were major developments in the theory of organizational behavior and in the effects of these behavioral considerations on management. Murdick and Ross[19] list six schools of present day organization and management theory. The factor that

[17] Henri Fayol, *General and Industrial Management,* Pitman, London, 1949.

[18] Frederick W. Taylor, *The Principles of Scientific Management,* Harper & Row, 1911.

[19] R. G. Murdick and J. E. Ross, *Information Systems for Modern Management,* Prentice-Hall, 1971, pp. 32-101.

[20] D. S. Pugh, D. J. Hickson and C. R. Hinings, *Writers on Organization,* Penguin Books, 1971.

should concern us here, however, is the degree to which these schools concern themselves with the use of quantitative measures and data in the practice of management.

It is not the purpose of the development of information systems to convert all organizations to the more quantitative forms of management, but rather to serve that portion of the management of an organization that relies on quantitative data. The information system must therefore serve and follow the philosophy of management in the organization in which it exists. Nevertheless, the provision of timely and meaningful quantitative information is likely to influence managers toward the quantitative aspects of management. However, the converse is true also; a bad implementation of an information system is likely to cause managers to avoid these quantitative aspects. Good management involves a combination of quantitative and qualitative factors and a good information system is one that unobtrusively serves the whole management process.

Centralization and Decentralization

A major issue in establishing the management policy in any organization is the degree of centralization and decentralization of responsibility for decision making. This has a major influence on the design of an information system, because that design must necessarily follow the pattern of decision making in the organization.

The issue of centralization or decentralization of authority was discussed at length by Alfred P. Sloan in his account of management problems in General Motors.[21] The position generally held today is that, whereas planning, budgeting and overall evaluation are best directed, or at least coordinated, centrally, the amount of authority over operations that should be delegated depends on the degree of initiative required at the scene of those operations. For example, considerable initiative is required by those carrying out research or artistic activities, and it would be inappropriate for each decision concerning these activities to be referred to higher authority. On the other hand, there is a need for the overall planning and evaluation of these activities by those not immediately engaged in the work. At the other end of the spectrum, the majority of decisions required on a standard production line are routine and can be made the subject of a manual of operating procedures. This type of operation is therefore much more amenable to centralized control.

In most organizations, there are activities that are directed

[21]Alfred P. Sloan, *My Years with General Motors,* Doubleday, 1963.

centrally and others for which responsibility is delegated. The information system must follow the chosen pattern of management, furnishing information pertinent to decision making at the locations where the decisions are made.

Discussion Topics

1/ Comment on the statement that the purpose of an organization is to create outputs from input resources.

2/ Do organizations exhibit adaptive behavior? How is this adaptive behavior related to homeostatic processes in organizations?

3/ What factors may contribute to a reduction in the purposefulness of an organization? What measures are necessary to counter the effect of these factors?

4/ Are multiple objectives in an organization necessarily a bad thing? When does an objective become a constraint on other members of a set of multiple objectives?

5/ If you were the Chief of the local fire department, what would be your overt objectives for the department? Would you have any covert objectives?

6/ What would be your program structure for the fire department?

7/ What is the relationship between program budgeting and responsibility reporting? Do both methods of management of resources have a place in an organization?

8/ How do requirements for program budgeting and responsibility reporting reflect on the desirable characteristics of an information system?

9/ Compare the usefulness in management of measures of effectiveness and measures of efficiency.

10/ What are the advantages and disadvantages of "proxy" measures of effectiveness?

11/ How should support functions be treated in the budgetary process?

12/ What is the relationship between "management by objectives" and program budgeting?

3

Decision Making

Decision making is one of the key roles of management. Herbert A. Simon goes so far as to say that he will "... find it convenient to take mild liberties with the English language by using 'decision making' as if it were synonomous with 'managing'."[1] Without necessarily accepting so broad a statement, it is, however, clear that an information system designed to serve management must be vitally concerned with the pattern of decision making in the organization.

The nature of decision making has been described by Simon,[1] C. W. Churchman,[2] and by a number of other authors.[3,4,5] Building on

[1]Herbert A. Simon, *The New Science of Decision Making,* Harper & Row, 1948, p. 1.

[2]C. West Churchman, *Prediction and Optimal Decision,* Prentice Hall, 1961.

[3]Samuel Eilon, "What is a Decision?", Management Science Vol. 16, No. 4, Dec. 1969.

[4]Wayne Lee, *Decision Theory and Human Behavior,* Wiley, 1971.

[5]J. von Neumann and O. Morgenstern, *Theory of Games and Economic Behavior,* Princeton University Press, 1953.

these descriptions, the steps in the decision making process may be listed as follows:

- Perception and formulation of the problem

- Construction of a model of the decision process

- Establishment of quantitative measures of variables involved in the process

- Definition of strategies or alternative courses of action

- Calculation of outcomes for the alternative courses of action

- Establishment of criteria for choice between courses of action

- Resolution or decision.

These steps should not be regarded as separate and independent. In practice there is considerable overlap between them. Neither is the sequence of steps rigid and unchangeable. In many cases, the decision is reached by an iterative procedure involving repetition of all or some of the steps. The actual procedure used depends to some extent on the methods adopted by the individual decision maker in the particular situation. Nevertheless, all the above steps must be observed implicitly or explicitly in arriving at a decision. A similar model of the decision process has been put forward by Eilon.[3]

Many of the above steps do not need much further explanation. The first, for example, refers to the need to separate out the issue requiring resolution from surrounding material, stating explicitly the matter to be resolved. Issues to which the decision is related are considered at this stage. Proper attention to this step in the process avoids solving the wrong problem and also some of the detrimental consequences of sub-optimization mentioned earlier. Omond Solandt[6] has given some interesting examples of the need to discover the real problem before proceeding to the later stages of decision making.

Once the problem has been formulated, it is necessary to construct a model representing it. Care must be taken that the model truly describes the situation under study and includes all the factors likely to affect the decision. The temptation to construct a model which provides an easy mathematical solution must be resisted if

[3]Samuel Eilon, "What is a Decision?", Management Science Vol. 16, No. 4, Dec. 1969.

[6]Omond Solandt, "Observation, Experiment and Measurement in Operations Research," Journal of the Operations Research Society of America, Vol. 3, No. 1, Feb. 1955.

there is any chance that the mathematics does not truly represent the process being studied. The temptation is particularly strong to adapt a general purpose model to a new application, for the reason that methods of solution are well known and readily available. As a simple example, there is a well known law that connects the time taken for a stone to fall to the water with the height of the cliff from which it is dropped. This is a perfectly satisfactory model for most experiments with stones. However, if the effects of air resistance, buoyancy and air-foils had been neglected in the model, it would make a very bad basis for studying the dropping of feathers.

Having devised the model, it is necessary to establish quantitative units in which the parameters involved will be expressed. In management decision models these are primarily the measures of effectiveness, efficiency and use of resources already discussed. It bears repeating here, that this is one of the most difficult of the steps in the process and one which is most often left incomplete when time for making a decision is limited. Whenever possible, actual measurements of the parameters involved should be used. In many cases, however, this is not possible and the only resort is to estimates of values determined from the best available experience and a process of thoughtful extrapolation.

In recent years, substantial progress has been made toward providing models which allow factual and quantitative data to be used in decision making in more and more complex situations. The science of operational research is devoted to this and has aided in the understanding of such phenomena as queues, scheduling of production machinery and inventory control.

Definition of strategies or alternatives provides the decision maker with a list of options available to him, the outcomes of which are then calculated using the model of the situation under review. Assuming that some criteria for choice between the outcomes have been established, the decision maker can proceed towards a resolution of the problem.

As mentioned earlier, these steps are frequently intermixed and resolution is obtained only after a number of iterations through the process. Furthermore, as time progresses, the whole nature of the process may change. It is wise, therefore, to check the validity of a process used previously when approaching what appears to be a similar situation after a lapse of time.

Rationality and Personalistic
Involvement in Decision Making

In the above discussion of the decision process, the major question of selection of criteria for choice between options was left for later discussion. It is, in fact, a central point in the study of how decisions are made. It is not our purpose here to consider this in detail, but rather to discuss how it affects the requirements placed on an information system to assist in the decision making process of an organization.

One concept at issue is that of *rationality* in decision making. Rationality is concerned with the manner in which the decision is made, given the evaluation of options and a choice of criteria for selection. Eilon[3] defines a restricted form of rational behavior in decision making saying:

> What I mean by rational resolution is that the decision maker conforms to the selection criteria; namely that if after applying the criterion, a course of action A is shown to be superior to B, the decision maker does in fact select A in preference to B. If he does not, then the resolution is irrational.

Another basic concept, that of personalistic involvement, is related to rationality and concerns the steps in the decision process prior to resolution. Eilon points out that in any given decision process, an individual decision maker may select a criterion for choice, depending on his judgment at the time. He states:

> If the decision maker is responsible for the criterion of choice, the decision process is personalistic in character, namely the resolution at the end of the process becomes a function of the decision maker's own personality, his beliefs, his attitudes and his value judgments. His resolution for given circumstances may well be different from that of another individual, though both may still behave rationally by our definition. If, on the other hand, the decision maker does not participate in the determination of a choice criterion, the decision process is *impersonalistic* and the outcome must be the same for different decision makers, if they all behave rationally.

The distinction between personalistic and impersonalistic decision making processes is of very great significance in the design of an

---

[3]Samuel Eilon, "What is a Decision?", *Management Science,* Vol. 16, No. 4, Dec. 1969.

information system. It is clear from Eilon's statement that the decision process which is personalistic can be specified in detail only so far as it relates to a particular person. A different person would proceed in a different manner. The best that an information system can do in these circumstances, therefore, may be to provide the decision maker with as much relevant information as possible without infringing on his desire to make the decision on the basis of his personality, beliefs, attitudes and judgments.

In the case of an impersonalistic decision process, however, the decision maker does not participate in determining the criteria for choice *at the time at which the decision is made.* The impersonalistic decision process can therefore be *completely specified* beforehand and rational behavior in resolution will always lead to the same decision. This type of decision is usually, but not always, found in the middle and lower levels of an organization involved in procedures that have become routine.

As a simple example of a decision process that can be completely specified, consider the resolution of the question "is 5 greater than 4?" In this case, the problem has been formulated and a model established in early schooling in arithmetic. The parameters with which the model deals are entirely quantitative and the criteria on which the decision is to be made are already established and agreed. The decision process is impersonalistic and rational resolution of the question will always provide the answer "yes, 5 is greater than 4."

If, however, the question is modified to read "are 5 oranges better than 4 apples," new considerations have been introduced that are not included in the simple decision process used to answer the original question. The basic problem is that 5 oranges and 4 apples are not directly comparable. What is required is a measure of the value of each of these alternatives in the situation confronting the decision maker. One approach to this problem is to attempt to estimate the *utility*[5,7] of 5 oranges compared to that of 4 apples as perceived by the decision maker. This is the equivalent of determining the usefulness of the alternatives to the decision maker in the situation confronting him. The decision has therefore become personalistic, because resolution is a function of ". . . the decision maker's own personality, his beliefs, his attitudes and his value judgments."[3]

[5]J. von Neumann and O. Morgenstern, *Theory of Games and Economic Behavior,* Princeton University Press, 1947.

[7]Wayne Lee, *Decision Theory and Human Behavior,* Wiley, 1971.

Unless an agreed upon scale of utility can be established, to which all who must make decisions of this type adhere, the decision process cannot be regarded as completely specified. Without this common measure of utility, two different persons, each acting rationally, may make different decisions.

Many situations arise in management in which agreed scales of utility cannot be established within the time available for decision making. These decisions cannot, therefore, be completely specified and the resolution is left to the individual decision maker, who uses his judgment on the basis of all the non-quantified (or qualitative) factors of which he is aware and all the quantitative information that can be made available to him.

Consider, for example, the problem of selecting an employee for a job. There are a number of factors that can be written down in simply stated form; age, number of dependents, present salary, formal education, etc. These can be used to select likely candidates from a list of applicants. The final decision is, however, usually taken only after an interview, in which qualities and characteristics that cannot be simply codified are reviewed. The selection is then made on the basis of both the codified information and the qualitative factors revealed in the interview using the judgment of the decision maker.

Sisson and Canning[8] have estimated that 80% to 90% (by *number*) of the decisions made in a business organization can be completely specified (they call this "computable"). They go on to say, however, that 60% to 80% of the decisions, by *type,* are of a sort that are not directly computable and that involve human judgment.

It would not be correct to omit mention in this discussion of rationality and personalistic involvement in decision making of the *principle of bounded rationality* put forward by Herbert A. Simon.[9] This principle can be interpreted as stating that in some administrative situations, some decision makers take into account only those factors that they regard as most relevant and crucial. To quote Simon:

> While economic man maximizes—selects the best alternative from among all those available to him, his cousin, whom we shall call

---

[8]R. L. Sisson and R. G. Canning, *A Manager's Guide to Computer Processing,* Wiley, 1967, p. 9.

[9]Herbert A. Simon, *Administrative Behavior,* The Free Press, New York, 1965, pp. xxiv-xxxiii.

administrative man, *satisfices*—looks for a course of action that is satisfactory or 'good enough.' "[9]

The principle of bounded rationality as stated by Simon bears mainly on how decisions with personalistic involvement are made. It is therefore peripheral to the main discussion in this chapter of the distinction between personalistic and impersonalistic decision processes. However, there is no doubt that satisficing occurs in impersonalistic decision processes *at the stage of specifying the quantitative parameters and the selection criteria to be used.* It is therefore an important concept in the work of design of completely specified decision processes, which is discussed in later chapters.

Completely Specified Decision Processes

A completely specified decision process has been described in the previous section as a decision process in which there is no personalistic involvement in the decision *at the time at which it is made.* This is not to say, however, that the appropriate managers should not be involved in the writing of the specifications for such a decision process. The characteristic that distinguishes a completely specified decision process from one in which there is personalistic involvement in the resolution is that the model, the quantified parameters, and the criteria for choice can be specified beforehand. These specifications can then be used in resolution as long as those with responsibility for the decision process continue to agree that they are valid. It follows from this that the specifications should be reviewed from time to time to check that they still apply to the situation under examination. This is particularly necessary in cases where the external environment and internal conditions in the organization are continually changing. Reviews of this nature should be undertaken in the normal course of management.

Completely specified decision processes are associated mainly with the middle and lower levels of management, where many decisions can be reduced to formal procedures. Examples are found in the routine processing of accounts and payroll, ordering and distribution of supplies and the handling of personnel information. These correspond to the "vertical systems" defined by Dearden in his

[9]Herbert A. Simon, *Administrative Behavior,* The Free Press, New York, 1965, pp. xxiv-xxxiii.

early article on the organization of information systems.[10] The decisions involved in these systems may be trivial in many cases. For example, "John Smith is paid \$3.50 per hour, he worked 37 hours last week, he incurred certain deductions of tax, pension fund contributions, health care premiums, etc.; what should be the amount of his check?" They are, nonetheless, decisions that are essential to the operation of the organization, as John Smith may tell you forcibly if you get his check wrong! The decision processes are *completely specified* because the model, quantitative parameters and criteria for resolution are agreed upon and remain in force until an external condition (for example, a tax change) forces a revision.

In many cases a series of trivial decisions, or calculations, can result in the resolution of a non-trivial problem. For example, the optimum allocation of resources to a range of manufacturing processes can be studied by linear programming.[11] In this case the model is complex, but it can be solved by a sequence of simple calculations and decisions. The involvement of management is in the initial setting up of the model, agreeing on the range of quantitative parameters to be studied, and specifying the meaning of the word "optimum." Once this has been done, the process will provide solutions for as long as management agrees it is valid.

The Role of the Computer in Decision Making

The program of instructions which controls the operation of a computer consists of a sequence of steps designed to solve the problem or support the procedure at hand. Some of these steps refer to the introduction of data into the processing, others are concerned with operations on these data, and some are concerned with the preparation and presentation of results from these operations. The sequence must be logical and consistent, but it is not necessarily purposeful. It is quite possible to instruct a computer to produce logical and consistent nonsense. The degree of purpose in a computer program depends on how faithfully the program represents a procedure which itself has purpose.

The requirement for consistency and logic in a computer program dictates that the decision processes involved be completely specified when the program is written. The decision making involved is

[10]John Dearden, "How to Organize Information Systems," Harvard Business Review, March-April 1965, pp. 19-27.

[11]Harvey A. Wagner, *Fundamentals of Operations Research,* Prentice-Hall, 1969, Chapter 4.

impersonalistic and rational, in the sense of the Eilon definition. The computer is well suited, therefore, to the support of completely specified administrative and operational procedures involved in management. This is not to say that all completely specified procedures in management should automatically be placed on a computer. Many such procedures can be undertaken more economically and more efficiently by staff members. On the other hand, when the volume of data is greater than can be handled by one or two persons, when the intricacy of the sequence of steps in the process exceeds their capability or when the volume of output to be produced is greater than their capacity, mechanization of the process using computers or data processing machines is desirable and usually economical.

Completely specified systems form a major part of the structured, or formal, component of the information system in most organizations. These completely specified systems serve administrative functions and operations in the organization. In many cases, these systems are mechanized and computer-supported and are commonly referred to as "data processing." Computer support of administrative and operational procedures in an organization is very similar to the control of production processes in industry. It is commonplace today to see production lines controlled by computer. Specifications for such processes as metal cutting and control of nuclear power generators can be determined in advance and programmed into the process control computer. Intervention by humans is required only when the specifications of the process are exceeded, either by a malfunction or by some other internal or external effect. If the process is to be changed in any respect, a new specification and a new computer program is prepared by personnel skilled in the area.

Computer programs prepared for the mechanization of administrative and operational processes must therefore comprise:

1/ A means of gathering internal and external data appropriate to the process.

2/ A specification of the process.

3/ Details of the outputs of the process.

4/ A means of summarizing the progress of the process during operations.

The program can then run unattended by management until either external conditions require a change in specifications of the process, or summary data on progress indicate that the process should be stopped or modified.

The summary data on progress can be programmed to appear at what may be called an *interface* with the system, and which is analogous to the gauges and dials which are monitored in process control. One portion of this summary data is useful to those engaged in monitoring the function itself and ensuring, for example, that the correct number of checks has been printed. The other portion of data appearing at the interface is the information which may be useful in other functions in the management of the organization; for example, the total number of employees and the total amounts paid as salary in the current pay period. The greater part of the data involved in any one system remains within the system itself and is concerned in the production of the outputs. The summary data at the interface allows managers to monitor progress and to combine results of one process with those from another.

Mechanization of administrative and operational processes affords a means of relieving managers of involvement in routine decisions and of leaving them freer to exercise their judgment in more complex situations. On the other hand, it is most undesirable to attempt to mechanize decision processes that are not impersonalistic and cannot be completely specified. This would be a denial of the requirement to involve managers in situations where their judgment is essential to the decision processes. The support provided by the computer to decision processes which are not completely specified should be limited to capture and processing of data, calculating outcomes where an agreed model exists and displaying the results of adopting a range of alternative courses of action. The final stages in the decision process should be left to the decision maker, who resolves the question in a personalistic fashion, which may or may not be rational. The question of whether his decision is rational, or not, is of interest to management but of no concern to those engaged in designing and implementing the information system.

The ideal situation is reached when large quantities of routine work are delegated to the computer and the nonroutine decisions are dealt with by the manager. The manager also has the responsibility of ensuring that the specifications of his mechanized systems are kept current in the light of the internal and external conditions under which he is operating.

Discussion Topics

1/ Do you agree with Herbert A. Simon in his contention that "decision-making is synonymous with managing"?

2/ It is relatively easy to apply the Eilon definition of rationality to the resolution stage of decision making. How does the concept of rationality apply to the selection of criteria for choice?

3/ How does pursuit of personal objectives affect rational behavior in decision making?

4/ What are the functions of the interface in a computer-supported completely specified system?

5/ Is the analogy between process control and the operations of completely specified administrative and operational systems tenable and useful?

6/ How are the completely specified systems related to the homeostatic process in an organization?

4

Measurements, Data, and Information

The foregoing discussions of quantitative aspects of management and decision making have stressed the need for data and information derived from measurements, but have not approached the question of why this need exists. The need arises, in fact, in management situations where it is necessary to communicate in other than general terms. As Churchman says, "Measurements are used when we feel the need for making 'fine' distinctions."[1]

It is implicit in Churchman's statement that the measurements must be relevant to the distinctions sought. In a study of three companies published in 1961,[2] Daniel concludes:

In retrospect, it is obvious that these three companies were plagued by a common problem—inadequate management informa-

[1] C. West Churchman, *Prediction and Optimal Decision,* Prentice-Hall, 1961, pp. 93-136.

[2] D. Ronald Daniel, "Management Information Crisis," Harvard Business Review, September-October 1961, pp. 91-101.

tion. The data were inadequate, not in the sense of there not being enough, but in terms of relevancy for setting objectives, for shaping alternative strategies, for making decisions and for measuring results against planned goals.

Daniel goes on to discuss the need for measurements in areas which have been referred to earlier as planning, direction of operations and evaluation. Churchman states, more generally, that measurements are required ". . . when we want to employ results obtained in one circumstance . . . in totally different circumstances."[1] The potential product of a measurement process is, therefore, information that will have a bearing on a decision process, either in planning, directing operations or evaluating results.

It is important that measurements should be made of all parameters that bear on the decision process in question. Decisions made on the measurement of use of resources alone are inadequate in many management situations, although this basis for decision making is in wide-spread use in present day organizations. For example, it is not uncommon for the manager whose use of funds exceeds budgeted figures to be regarded with some disapproval, while the man who does not spend all of the allocated amounts is thought of as a good, thrifty manager. These judgments are based on the assumption that the resources allocated were just the right amount for the job. It is possible, however, that the manager who overspent, obtained proportionately greater benefits for each unit of resources expended than the man who kept well within his budget. His overspending was counter to the need for *control* of expenditures in the organization, but was nevertheless more productive in terms of achieving its objectives. Measurements of the benefits accruing to the organization in this case might therefore point to the need for allocating more funds to the more successful manager and less to the one who underspent his budget.

This conclusion would not be apparent in the case described if measurements of benefits had not been made in addition to measurements of use of resources. A substantial proportion of the decisions required in management is of the type in which benefits are compared to use of resources. The method by which these two types of parameters are measured is therefore most important in the design of an information system.

---

[1]C. West Churchman, *Prediction and Optimal Decision,* Prentice-Hall, 1961, pp. 93-136.

The Methodology of Measurement

Churchman has described three aspects of measurement as:

1/ Specification of what is being measured.

2/ Selection of a standard language describing what is being measured.

3/ Establishment of standards of accuracy and control of measurements.[1]

A similar treatment of the basic aspects of measurement has been given by Morgenstern.[3]

In the context of management, *what* is to be measured consists mainly of parameters relating to use of resources and accomplishment of goals and objectives. With respect to resources, these measurements may relate to employment of personnel on staff, expenditure of money, use of personnel on contract, use of machines, facilities, lands and buildings, and consumption of resource materials from direct supply or inventory. Specification of measures of accomplishment of goals and objectives in general terms is more difficult because these measures must relate to the aspirations and objectives of individual organizations. The reader is asked to refer back to the discussion of quantitative measures of effectiveness and efficiency in Chapter 2.

One further class of parameters which may need to be measured refers to standards and constraints imposed on the organization both from outside and by internal policies. Provisions of union contracts are an example of the former, and salaries scales for management fall into the latter category. The need to measure these parameters is normally imposed on the organization rather than created within it. The crucial factor with regard to these parameters, as with all others treated by the information system, is the *unit* in which they are measured.

The establishment of standard units of measurement of all parameters is an essential preliminary task in the design of an information system. In North America we are all used to thinking of the dollar as the standard unit for measuring the parameter

---

[1] C. West Churchman, *Prediction and Optimal Decision,* Prentice-Hall, 1961, pp. 93-136.

[3] Oskar Morgenstern, *On the Accuracy of Economic Observations*, Princeton University Press 1970, Chapter VII, pp. 117-127.

"money." If we wish to consider any other measure of money, such as the pound sterling, there is a standard algorithm (the exchange rate) which relates the new measure back to the dollar. Use of personnel is thought of in man hours or perhaps man years, use of machines in hours, and use of buildings in square feet and time. The tendency is to convert all use of such resources to dollars in the process of allocation and budgeting by use of standard conversion rules; for example, $6.50 per year per square foot of building space. This is natural and convenient when the resource can be quickly bought with money. Difficulties arise when such purchases involve considerable lead time, such as may be the case with special purpose buildings and machines. In these cases, a separate quantitative measure may be necessary for use in allocating the scarce resource.

Measures of achievement of goals and objectives are less easily converted into a single parameter, since they may be related to widely differing areas of activity. The concept of *utility*, referred to in Chapter 3, is an attempt to combine various measures of effectiveness into a single parameter related to the objectives of the decision maker. When a manager uses "judgment" in resolving a decision process it can be said that he implicitly assigns a utility to the various outcomes. If he acts rationally, he chooses the alternative that maximizes utility to him.

There is a danger in rigid adherence to a single measure of utility that the key value judgments which went into construction of the measure will be forgotten with the passage of time. This danger is particularly strong when priorities and objectives are changing. If a single utility measure is adopted, its basis should be reviewed continually and the constituent measures of achievement of objectives retained for future use.

It is particularly important that the measures of resources and achievement of objectives should be standard throughout the organization. This is not to say that different organizational sub-units working toward different objectives should necessarily adopt the same measures of effectiveness and efficiency. What is important is that different sub-units working toward the *same* objective adopt the same measures of use of resources and achievement. This allows the manager responsible for the sub-units to compare their achievements and to make a judgment on their effectiveness and efficiency, taking into account all other factors (and constraints) bearing on the situation. Whereas in most cases the manager will not wish to make his judgment on the quantitative factors alone, provision of measures of achievement and use of resources for the different sub-units in the same terms will provide him with a quantitative basis from which he can proceed to his judgment by incorporating the other, more qualitative, factors involved.

Accuracy and *control* are the factors that define the consistency of measurements. As Churchman says[1], in the standard environment, the reports generated according to a set of specifications may not all be exactly alike. In management, this often arises from different interpretations of the set of specifications. As a simple example, if an executive travels to another city and entertains a customer at dinner, is the cost of his dinner a travel or an entertainment expense? Differences of interpretation in more complex cases can have a significant effect on the accuracy of measurements. Control of accuracy consists of deciding when to test the accuracy of measurements and what to do if some remedial action is judged necessary. In this regard, consistency, though desirable, is not necessarily a synonym for accuracy.

Data and Information

Data result from measurements. However, unless data are placed in context and presented to the appropriate decision maker, the effort of measurement may be wasted. When data are placed in context, they may be said to have become information. Quoting Churchman, once again, "It should be noted that by 'information' we mean recorded experience which is useful in decision making."[1]

Information may therefore be regarded as that which decreases uncertainty in a decision process. The amount by which uncertainty is decreased depends upon the probability of the information being presented; that is to say, the less probable the message, the more information it gives.[4] If man bites dog, that is news. The usefulness of information therefore depends on the amount of "news" it contains, so that repetition of the same management information month after month in a periodic reporting system is not likely to be very useful. True, it could be said that no news is good news, that the absence of useful information shows that the plan is being followed faithfully. The danger is that managers may come to ignore the reports and consequently miss an important deviation from the values that have come to be expected. Establishment of reporting by exception (and acceptance of this by managers) ensures that information reported has lower probability of occurring and there-

[1]C. West Churchman, *Prediction and Optimal Decision,* Prentice-Hall, 1961, pp. 93-136.

[4]Norbert Wiener, *The Human Use of Human Beings,* Avon Books, 1967, p. 31.

fore higher usefulness in decision making.

Because it is possible to interpret information as a measure of organization, in the sense that entropy is a measure of disorganization, an increase of information useful in decision making can be thought of as contributing to the purposefulness of an organization. However, information that is ignored by decision makers does not make any such contribution. For this reason, the best designed information system which does not have the confidence of managers and is not used by them, will make little or no contribution to the effectiveness of an organization.

Aggregation of Data

Aggregation occurs when two or more pieces of data are combined to form a new piece of data; for example when the expenditures in some category by one organizational sub-unit are combined with those of another. Aggregation therefore results in a reduction of the amount of data but not necessarily a reduction in information. When the expenditures of the two units combined are required in the context of a decision, there is no loss of information. If in another context, however, the expenditures of both units were required and only aggregated data were available, a loss of information relative to the new context would have taken place.

March and Simon have described a process that they call "uncertainty absorption."[5] This occurs when a series of decisions or actions take place at one level in an organization and only inferences drawn from those decisions and actions are reported to a higher level. Aggregation of data cause uncertainty absorption in this sense, in that inferences drawn from the data are reported, i.e., the sum of the expenditures of the two units, rather than the raw data.

Aggregation of data in a completely specified decision process is permissible because it can be assumed that the manner of aggregation, and the nature of the uncertainty absorption, has been determined and agreed beforehand. A problem may arise, however, if the raw data are discarded at the time of aggregation. Suppose for example that data are aggregated in a decision process, but that at a later time another decision is required which requires use of the data in unaggregated form. Information may have been lost if the raw data is not recoverable. This could occur if all salaries and wages in an organization are calculated by union affiliation and then summed,

[5] James G. March and Herbert A. Simon, *Organizations*, Wiley, 1958, p. 165.

discarding the individual union totals. The next time a union negotiation occurs, the salaries and wages paid to its members may be an important piece of information, which would not be recoverable if the original data had not been retained.

We may conclude, therefore, that aggregation of data in an information system is allowable and, in fact, necessary, in order to reduce the amount of data processed. Further, the raw data should be retained until it is beyond doubt that they will not be required in future decision processes or in planning studies. These data may be retained in a relatively low cost store (such as on magnetic tape or microfilm), which in automatic data processing is the analogue of a filing cabinet or dead storage location.

In retaining raw data over long periods of time, it is important to store alongside them the definitions and specifications referring to them. Ideas and definitions tend to change and it is not sufficient to rely on the memories of those involved, who may even have left the organization, to relate old data to present day specifications. Once standards of data definitions have been established, any change in these standards should be carefully documented and a method of conversion from the old to the new placed on record. If possible, important segments of stored data should be converted at the time of the change in specification.

By this method, a historic store of data relevant to the operations of the organization will be built up which will be invaluable in planning future activities. This store should be continually reviewed and portions that are judged to have lost their relevance discarded. This procedure, which is normally followed in dealing with papers stored in filing cabinets, will prevent the cost of the historic data store from becoming too high. Without the historic store, recreation of data in an organization for more than two years back is seldom possible from what records remain. Further recovery is usually impossible due to the effects of aggregation and the shortness of memories of those handling data for which specifications have changed over the years.

Standards in Data Representation

Just as humans need a standard language with which to communicate their ideas and thoughts, the information system must be based on a set of definitions and formats of data and information which is standard throughout the organization. Without such a set of standards, communication via the information system would be very difficult, if not impossible.

We have already seen the need for standard definitions of measures of resources and achievement of objectives, which are understood and accepted by all who need to use them. These definitions should be written so as to allow the minimum freedom for interpretation. This is difficult enough when only the English language is involved. When use of a second language, such as French, is necessary and an exact correspondence is required between descriptive definitions in the two languages, the problem is much more difficult.

A similar problem arises in standardizing the representation of data when all, or part, of the information system is computer-supported. In order to reduce storage space and processing requirements, certain classes of data and descriptions are coded in a shorter and more convenient form. Unless the coding conventions are standardized, they can represent a substantial barrier to communication between different portions of the information system. This seemingly simple requirement can present major difficulties in practice. There is a story about a committee set up to integrate a number of systems processing personnel data. Among the first descriptions to be standardized were surname, given names, age and other personal details. At the start, there were four different conventions that had been adopted to represent the surname, for a variety of reasons, but mainly to conserve space. This was resolved fairly easily. When it came to describing the sex of an individual, this seemed easy too; an M for male and F for female was suggested. The data processing expert pointed out however, that 1 for male and 0 for female would require less storage space. A lady member of the committee then suggested 0 for male and 1 for female. Yet another member said that sometimes the sex of a new employee was not immediately known (if his or her name was Jean, for example). An "unknown" category was required in addition to male and female.

This simple example illustrates the difficulty in constructing a standard language for automated data processing systems. Computer-supported systems that have been created in different parts of an organization at different times and under different administrative control are most unlikely to have been written around a common set of data and descriptor coding conventions. Construction of such standards is therefore a first task in the implementation of an information system. This work is tedious, long and seemingly unproductive. Without it, however, the degree of communication between components of the system will be drastically reduced.

At a higher level, unless standard descriptions of categories of information are agreed and adhered to, there is a danger that an individual manager may place a personal interpretation on the information provided to him. This is the equivalent of his absorbing uncertainty about the information. A certain amount of this is inevitable in practice. If it becomes widespread, however, the recipient of inferences or of decisions based on the information will be limited in his capability to judge the correctness of what is passed to him and the usefulness of the information system will deteriorate.

Discussion Topics

1/ How would you describe "information" in the context of management information systems? Are there different categories of such information, and are there sub-sets of data in organizations that are excluded from your description?

2/ Discuss the possibility of a relationship between the effective use of information in an organization, its purposefulness and organizational entropy.

3/ How would you go about establishing measures of effectiveness for inclusion in an information system? What would be your criteria for selection of such measures?

4/ How does Churchman's statement that "measurements must be relevant to the distinctions sought" bear on the requirements for an information system?

5/ How is aggregation of data related to "uncertainty absorption" as described by March & Simon (*Organizations,* Wiley, 1958, p. 165)?

6/ What are desirable characteristics of a historic store of data in an organization? How should such a store be administered?

5

Components of an Information System

Having discussed the quantitative aspects of management and the nature of data and information in previous chapters, we may now proceed to an examination of the general characteristics of an information system.

The components of an information system are those parts of the organization concerned with the acquisition, processing, retention, transmission and presentation of information useful to management. In the treatment that follows they are described under the following headings:

- *Administrative and operational systems*, serving routine functions in the organization, such as personnel administration, production scheduling, etc.

- *The management reporting system*, which provides periodic and timely reports to managers on matters relating to their decision making tasks.

- *The common data base*, which acts as a store for data and information used by more than one part of the organization.

- *The information retrieval system*, by which historic data and information may be retrieved for use in planning and decision making.

- *The data management system*, which arranges and controls the flow of data and information between components of the information system.

A diagram showing the various components for an information system is given in Figure 5-1. This diagram is useful in understanding the relationship between the components of the system. It will be necessary also, in the discussion of the information flow in the system, which follows the description of the individual components.

The information system described in this chapter may be regarded

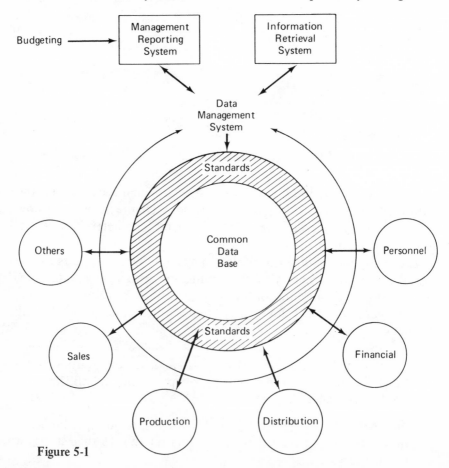

Figure 5-1

as the end result toward which the systems designer strives. In dealing with the desired end-product first, it is not intended to ignore the process of getting from "here" to "there," which may be long and arduous. The task of implementing a system based on the characteristics described here, and the difficulties that may be experienced, is covered in the following chapters.

The Administrative and Operational Systems

The administrative and operational systems are those components of the information system created to support routine functions in the organization. A typical listing of these functions and of sub-categories within these functions is shown in Table 5-1.

In most modern organizations, completely specified systems have been designed to process all or some of these routine functions. In many organizations, these systems are mechanized and computer-supported and are referred to as "data processing." In others, the functions have been reduced to routine procedures, which are undertaken or overseen by staff members. In some instances, the human being acts as a link between two or more sub-components of the function which have been completely specified and mechanized. The extent to which mechanization of these administrative and operational systems has taken place in an organization need not concern us until we come to consider implementation of an information system in the next chapter. Suffice it now to recognize that a number of routine administrative and operational functions exist in all organizations which can be completely specified and mechanized, if it is economic and desirable to do so.

Table 5-1
Typical Functions Served by Administrative
and Operational Systems

Personnel	:	maintenance of personnel records
	:	administration of pension plan(s)
	:	industrial relations
	:	other employee services
Finance	:	payroll
	:	accounts receivable and payable
	:	general ledger
	:	cost accounting
	:	internal audit
Distribution	:	scheduling and maintenance of inventories
	:	order control and shipping

Production   :   purchasing and procurement
                :   maintenance of inventories of resources
                :   production planning and control
                :   maintenance and equipment control
Sales   :   market research and product development
                :   sales planning and promotion
                :   order processing

The tasks undertaken in these completely specified systems are:

1/ Gathering of data related to the function from internal and external sources.

2/ Processing these data according to the details of the decision making processes which have been specified.

3/ Producing outputs necessary to the function.

4/ Producing data and information useful to other functions and to higher levels of management.

For example, an administrative system servicing the accounts payable function might gather data on the accounts to be paid, process these data against the procedures laid down in the organization for the payment of accounts, produce checks for mailing, and provide summaries of amounts paid for use by other parts of the organization.

Whether a completely specified system of this nature is mechanized, partly mechanized, or run by staff members, it is necessary that it be monitored to ensure that the operation is running according to the specifications. A built-in sub-component of the system therefore provides and displays such data on the progress of tasks underway as are required by the supervisor of operations. It may be that there are certain thresholds or limits in the process or in the input data beyond which operations according to the specifications are not satisfactory. The system therefore includes details of these thresholds and limits, together with descriptions of means of bringing any transgression to the notice of the operator or supervisor. This is the equivalent of setting up a *monitor* as an integral part of the operation. The data available at the monitor are such as to allow the operator to diagnose the cause of any anomaly in the operation and to take the necessary remedial action. A further category of data which can be provided at the monitor is that relating to assessments of the efficiency of the operation. This is useful to the manager of the function or operation in his reviews of performance and also for passage to other units for inclusion in complementary assessments of efficiency.

The greatest proportion of the data and information with which an administrative or operational system is concerned remains within that system and the routine functions that it serves. Some of the data and information in the system may, however, be of interest to other functions and to general management of the organization. For example, a system designed for scheduling the use of a certain facility implicitly contains information on the overall utilization of that facility that may be useful in planning future operations. The specifications for the system provide, therefore, for summary information of this nature to be available *explicitly* at what was referred to earlier as *interface,* from which it can be transferred to other parts of the organization. More detailed data and information needed by other administrative and operational systems (for example, lists of personnel on staff prepared in the personnel system to be passed to a financial system for payroll purposes) can also be specified to be available at the interface.

Considerable aggregation of input data takes place in an administrative or operational system. In order that the unaggregated data not be lost, the system specifications provide for its retention in a low-cost storage medium until it is judged that it can be discarded. Data and information appearing at the outputs of the system and at the interface are similarly retained. In order that these data are meaningful when retrieved at a later date, the context, timing and full description of the data are stored alongside them. A schematic diagram of one of the administrative or operational systems is shown in Figure 5-2.

Examples of these administrative and operational systems in a typical organization are shown as circles in the lower half of Figure 5-1. In many cases, these circles represent groups of systems as indicated by Table 5-1. Specifications of these systems are continually reviewed in order that all aspects may be kept in line with changing requirements and varying conditions inside and outside the organization.

The Management Reporting System

The purpose of the management reporting system, shown at the top left of Figure 5-1, is to present to managers at all levels in the organization reports that are useful to them in their day-to-day work of decision making. These reports fall into three categories:

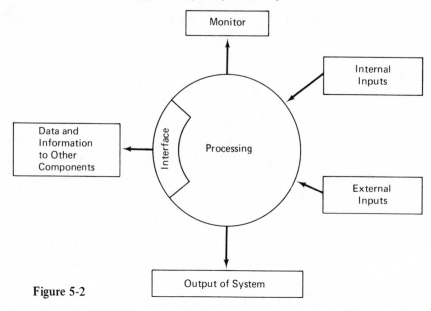

Figure 5-2

- Those required for *control* of use of resources.

- Reports relating to the *efficiency* of operations and management of resources.

- Reports relating to *effectiveness* in achieving goals and objectives as a function of resources expended.

Data and information required for the first two categories of reports are available within the administrative and operational systems and can be transferred via the interface on request. Data and information for the third category of reports can also be obtained via the interfaces. Before presentation in the third type of reports, data from the administration and operational systems is combined with information on budgeted goals and use of resources available directly from the budgeting function in the organization.

The proportion of reports required by an individual manager falling into any one of these categories depends upon the role and position of the manager in the organization, as does the degree of detail needed in the reports. For example, the manager of a particular resource, such as personnel, would presumably need very few reports in the third category. Most of the reports he requires are of the first and second kinds and these need to contain a considerable amount of detailed information. On the other hand, the executive vice-president who concerns himself with all aspects of the organization, requires reports of all three kinds. The degree of detail in reports directed to him, however, is much less than in the case of his subordinates, to whom he has presumably delegated most of the detailed tasks of management.

The structure of the management reporting system therefore follows the structure of the management process of the organization which it serves. In particular, the degree of detail of reporting at any level is dependent on the degree of true delegation of responsibility from the level which determines the pattern of decision making in the organization.

In the above discussion, the emphasis was on information *required* by managers in their decision making tasks. Information needed by managers as background to their day-to-day work is equally important. Much of this background can be acquired in informal exchanges such as occur in meetings, discussions and conferences. The formal reports of the management reporting system are limited to those collections of information that have been found from experience to be required *regularly* and *periodically* in the management process. The amount of information reported is the smallest quantity which meets the requirements of the managers concerned.

The reports comprising the management reporting system contain vital information on the efficiency and effectiveness of the organization and of its sub-units. For this reason, many of the reports may be confidential and, as such, they are presented, at least in the first instance, only to the managers directly concerned. The reports are made available simultaneously to superior and subordinate managers responsible for a function, operation or program element. They can then be discussed as necessary as part of the management process and decisions made regarding any action required. A manager responsible for a number of sub-units engaged in activities contributing toward the same objective can make useful comparisons if he receives reports in similar formats from his subordinates. Information, rather than action copies of the reports are sent to others only by agreement of the parties directly concerned.

In operation, the management reporting system provides timely and consistent reports following a previously agreed upon specification to the managers involved. The specifications for reports at each level in the organization cover detailed descriptions of information to be drawn from reports produced at lower levels and designate information to be summarized and reported to higher levels. The whole system of reports displays increasing summarization and corresponding absorption of uncertainty the higher the level in the organization.

As with the administrative and operational systems, a means for retention of both aggregated and unaggregated data in a historic store is provided, so that information required at a later date can be retained. As before, a review procedure by which data and information judged no longer useful can be discarded is a necessity.

The Common Data Base

The common data base is central to the whole information system. It is shown in Figure 5-1 surrounded by the administrative and operational systems on the one hand and by the management reporting system on the other. Conceptually speaking, it is connected to these systems by channels between it and the individual system interfaces. It does not, however, contain all data and information treated by these systems. Membership in the common data base is restricted to data and information common to two or more of these systems, including the management reporting system. The data and information in the common data base therefore concerns a wider range of activities in the organization than any one of the surrounding administrative and operational systems, which are restricted to a particular function or operation.

The majority of the data and information in any one of the administrative and operational systems remains within that system and need not necessarily conform to standards set up for the organization as a whole. *However, data and information passing between two or more of the administrative and operational systems or between any one of these systems and the management reporting system must be in standard format* in order that it be acceptable and recognizable to each system it enters. This is denoted in Figure 5-1 by the annular area marked "standards" between the peripheral systems and the common data base. By extension of this argument, if two or more parts of the organization are geographically separated or semi-autonomous within the management structure, each part may have its own information system and its own local common data base. Data and information that pass between two or more such parts of the organization are then included in a common data base for the organization as a whole.

In practice, the common data base tends to grow from a small beginning, rather than be created in one abrupt operation. This growth takes place as more and more interaction takes place between the administrative and operational systems and as the management reporting system assumes a more and more important role in the

internal communications of the organization. Both of these developments tend to create more and more candidates for inclusion in the
common data base and, consequently, a greater degree of standardization of data and information within the organization.

Due to the central position of the common data base in the
information system, and in the organization, its operation must be
strictly regulated. This is necessary to maintain the quality of the
data and information it contains and to ensure that they conform to
the standards which are established for entry. Unless strict control is
maintained, the quality of the contents soon deteriorates and what
has been established as a common source of information for the
whole organization degenerates into a series of groupings of data,
each of which is the private concern of one part of the organization.

Data and information that are candidates for entry to the base
come from systems previously under the administrative control of
one or other part of the organization. One aspect of this control is
jurisdiction over the quality of the information, the right to edit it,
and the right to decide when and how to update it. When data or
information are admitted to the common data base, these control
functions must be coordinated. This necessitates agreement between
administrators in those parts of the organization where the data or
information originates or where they are a vital part of some
administrative, operational or managerial system. Agreement may
not be easy to achieve if the various administrators have strong
partisan feelings about the ownership of "their" data.[1,2]

Transfer of data and information from the peripheral system to
the common data base may involve changes in administrative
procedures that have been established for some time. With good will
and cooperation between staff members, these changes can be
introduced as data and information are admitted to the base. Failure
to recognize the intimate connection between the data and information and the procedures for control, editing and updating can,
however, cause conflict and bad feeling. *This is a major reason for
gradual building of the data base*, taking due regard of the need to
establish new administrative procedures as part of the process.

Data and information in the common data base are continually
changing as a result of editing and updating. In the same manner as in
other parts of the information system, the administration of the data

---

[1]C. W. Harvison and K. J. Radford, "Creating a Common Data Base," Journal of Systems
Management, Vol. 23, No. 6, June 1972, pp. 8-12.

[2]Adrian M. McDonough, *Centralized Systems*, Thompson Book Co., Wayne, Pa., 1969, p.
100.

base must provide for the establishment of a historic store of its contents. This is also a good safeguard against loss or destruction of information that is vital to the organization, particularly if the historic store is contained in a separate location.

The Information Retrieval System

The information retrieval system, shown at the top right of Figure 5-1, has a function similar to that of the management reporting system, in that it provides information to all levels of management as required by them in their day to day tasks. Whereas the reports provided by the management reporting system are *structured* and *periodic*, the information retrieval system provides managers with the capability of obtaining information from the system on demand, in a form that is not structured in advance. Reports from the information retrieval system are provided when required and are therefore not periodic. However continual demand for a particular format of information is a good reason to suggest that this format be included in the output from the management reporting system.

It is not intended, in this conceptual treatment, to regard procedures for quick access to information on the current situation in an administrative or operational system as part of the information retrieval system. Facilities for this recovery of information are best designed into the specifications for the monitor function in those systems. The major use of the information retrieval system is to provide a relatively slower means of obtaining data and information which are required in planning and evaluation studies. However, small amounts of information may be required quickly by managers to answer questions and to provide background for their day-to-day work.

The Data Management System

The last major component of the information system is the data management system. This is needed to act as a link in communication between the other components, and it is diagrammed in Figure 5-1 as a circle surrounding the common data base, between it and the peripheral administrative, operational and reporting systems. The major tasks of the data management system are:

- Supervising the capture and updating of data and information for the common data base.

- Servicing the needs of the peripheral components of the system for data and information from the base.

- Maintaining a system of cross indexing of data currently in the information system as a whole.

- Generating reports in the formats required by the management reporting and information retrieval systems.

- Providing security for data in the base against accidental damage, intentional malice or inquisitiveness.

In large information systems, data management is usually undertaken using complex computer software. In small systems, and often in the early stages of implementation of large systems, the task can be accomplished by a small group of staff members.

Operation of the System

The operation of the information system may now be reviewed by reference to Figure 5-1. Routine administrative and operational functions are undertaken by completely specified systems which receive data and information from internal and external sources. The functioning of these systems is reviewed when necessary by the managers responsible for them on the basis of information available at a monitor. Data and information required by other functions or for reporting to other levels of management appear at interfaces in the peripheral systems, which are connected to the common data base. These data and information must conform to established standards in order to gain admittance to the base and to be passed from there to other components of the system. Reports for management are compiled from data and information in the common data base. Those which are structured and periodic are provided by the management reporting system; those which are not required periodically or have not been previously structured are provided on demand by the information retrieval system. Flow of data and information is controlled by a data management system. Data and information in the system which is subject to aggregation is placed in a historic store from which it can be retrieved, if this is found necessary, to support future decision processes. The contents of the common data base are also transferred regularly to a historic store to provide a continual record of the affairs of the organization and also to safeguard against loss or destruction of the current base.

The basic generic design is applicable to a system for the organization as a whole or to any portion of it. It may be that parts of an organization geographically separated or semi-autonomous in operation should set up their own information systems to the same general design, each with its own common data base. Data and information of common concern to two or more such parts of the organization, or to one part of the organization and the head office, are then exchanged between the common data bases. Under these circumstances, *the degree of formal communication achieved between the parts of the organization is in direct relation to the degree of standardization of data descriptions, formats and codes that has been achieved.*

This can be illustrated by the following diagram. At one end of the spectrum, the information systems in the various parts of the organization are completely independent: at the other end, one single system is used throughout the whole organization. The direction from left to right in the diagram is the direction of increasing standardization among the information systems in the various component parts of the organization. It is also the direction of increasing formal communication between those components through the medium of the information systems.

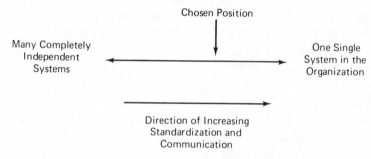

Figure 5-3

The problem of deciding what degree of standardization is required between components of the organization then resolves itself into determining the degree of communication required between them. A lesser degree of communication would lead to a chosen position to the left of the scale in Figure 5-3 and a greater degree to the right.

This conceptual description of an information system conforms closely to procedures in most well-organized entities. It allows for all necessary functions in an organization that were described in the earlier chapters. The design is based in some respects on a

Figure 5-4

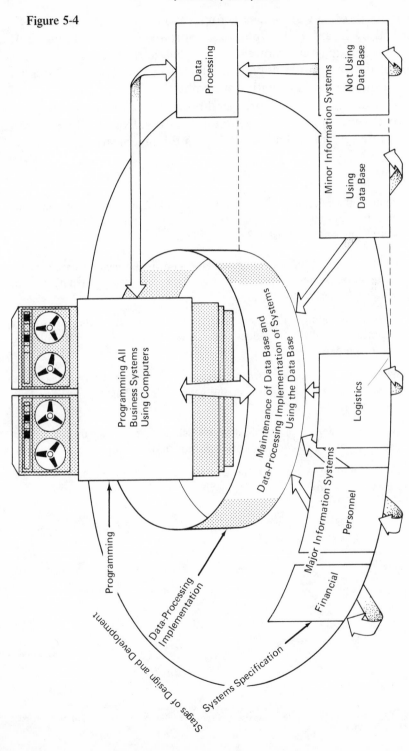

"generalized organization chart for systems and data processing" described by Dearden in 1965,[3] and reproduced here as Figure 5-4. This Dearden diagram, however, included a representation of the stages of design and development, which to some extent reduces its clarity as model for information system design.

Having described the desired end-product, it is now necessary to turn to the process of implementation, starting from the basis of the information system that already exists in the organization.

Discussion Topics

1/ What is the relationship between reports available from the management reporting system and those presented at the monitor function in a completely specified system?

2/ What is the role of the common data base in the generic design of an information system? How does this data base relate to data sets in completely specified systems?

3/ How is the common data base related to administrative procedures in an organization? What effect does this relation have on the work of building a common data base?

4/ What is the difference between the management reporting system and the information retrieval system in the generic design? Is this an important distinction?

5/ How is the degree of standardization achieved in setting up a common data base related to communication within an organization?

6/ How would you compare the generic design presented here with the Dearden diagram of 1965?

---

[3]John Dearden, "How to Organize Information Systems," Harvard Business Review, March-April, 1965.

6

Implementation of an Information System

In this chapter, we consider the implementation of an information system. This is not to be confused with the implementation of routine data processing applications, although these completely specified administrative and operational systems are important components of the information system. To quote H. S. Gellman,

> Management information systems do not come automatically as "by-products" of routine data processing systems. They do not even come as "products" unless careful, long range plans for information systems are developed at the outset, before the routine applications are implemented.[1]

The starting point of the implementation is the information

---

[1]H. S. Gellman, "EDP and MIS are not synonymous," Canadian Data Systems, November, 1969.

system that exists in the organization when the project is begun and which serves as a communications medium for management at that time. This existing information system may be rudimentary or it may be well developed in many respects. The problem is to move from the existing system to one based on the generic design described in the last chapter, with the minimum disruption of the management of the organization.

There are certain pre-conditions that must be satisfied before embarking on an implementation of this nature. These pre-conditions concern the awareness and attitudes of the senior management of the organization.

It is seldom wise to start the implementation of an information system unless senior management is aware that the existing system is inadequate and is prepared to commit itself to the solution of this problem. There has been a great deal written and said that might give senior managers the impression that any problems with an information system can be remedied swiftly and at a little extra expense by the acquisition of a new computer or a new software package. This may be true in some cases; but in the overwhelming majority of organizations, the solution is not as simple. What is needed, in most cases, is a systematic examination of the information flow as it relates to the decision making processes in the organization. This is seldom easy or cheap. It may reconfirm the existing information system as adequate in most respects. On the other hand, it may reveal requirements for change, not only in the existing information system, but also in the management process of the organization itself.

Senior management must be prepared, therefore, for an arduous reassessment of the organization's needs in information flow and decision making. Inevitably in such a process, there is some disturbance of established patterns and some opposition to proposed changes. *Unless or until senior management is prepared for this and also willing to commit resources to the project over a time period of between two to five years, it is unwise to start the implementation.*

The Existing Information System

The first step in the implementation is to examine in detail the information system already existing in the organization. This system is the one used by managers in their day-to-day work at the start of the implementation. Its characteristics provide valuable clues regarding the nature of the management processes and the flow of information in the organization.

It is unusual at the present time to find an organization in which the information system has been specifically planned and designed to meet the needs of management. In most cases, it has grown up with the organization. Reports that were found to be necessary on a recurring basis have become formalized in time and modified to meet changing circumstances. Information flow tends to be along channels established by previous contacts and practices.

As organizations have become more complex, there has been a tendency for managers to specialize. Some have specialized in the management of resources, such as money and personnel; others in operations, such as sales and production. With this increasing specialization, information has tended to be channeled along functional lines. For example, financial reporting systems and personnel reporting systems have been created which show in detail how the organization has fared in these particular functional areas. These systems are useful in the study and control of the particular resource to which the system refers. They are not so meaningful, however, for assessing the effectiveness of the organization in making progress towards the achievement of goals and objectives. Furthermore, systems created in different functional areas tend to be mutually inconsistent in small details; for example, data reported on the same activity may be slightly different or the time periods covered may vary.

Ironically enough, mechanization and the introduction of computer support for administrative and operational systems is one of the most common factors contributing to non-standardization and non-compatibility of data and information. Typically, computer support of systems is introduced piece-meal, application by application and department by department. At the time of mechanization of each particular system, conventions for parameter definition, data formats and coding are established and these are held standard for that application. In some cases, these standards do not seem to be appropriate for the next application; in others, they are completely ignored under the pressure to get the new system operational. It may even be that completely different teams of specialists work on applications in different parts of an organization with very little communication between them. When these applications are under separate or semi-autonomous administrative control, the need for standardization between the systems is not apparent, nor does it seem important compared with other pressing matters.

The result is that in many organizations a number of computer-based administrative and operational systems may exist which operate substantially independently of one another. Exchange of data and information between these systems is difficult and often requires interpretation, decoding and recoding of data. Even where two or more such systems use the same kind of data as part of their inputs, the data may be captured separately and recorded in different formats and codes. Until recently, for example, the Government of Canada had five different systems which used the list of all public servants in five different applications. These systems had been developed at different times and no standard list of employees was available. The file of employees created for one application could not be used in any other, because each system had been designed around the characteristics of the file chosen for the particular application. The task of creating a common employee list was immense, although a start was made by introducing an agreed upon set of specifications for a part of the file common to all applications.

As we have seen, it is common today that data and information that are basic to the operations of an organization are stored in more than one form in more than one location. Furthermore, these data and information may be under different administrative control in each different location. They may be updated and edited at different times and errors may exist in one set and not in another. This situation may not be a problem if the administrative and operational systems can exist truly independently. However, if these systems are used to provide data and information to be combined in a series of management reports, anomalies may arise that are beyond the capability or patience of a manager to correct. It is not surprising that one senior executive was heard to exclaim, "I know there is all kinds of information out there, but I can't seem to get my hands on it!"

Similar exasperation is often expressed by those involved in planning studies who need to recover data on past operations and activities of the organization. In many cases, only aggregated or summary data are available. Often in the process of mechanization, the need to maintain a historic store of data and information (the analogue of the filing cabinet) is forgotten.

The desire to maintain a personal store of information is one which remains strong in the face of the implementation of an organization-wide information system. Often this personal store is associated, by the manager concerned, with status in the organization and with the notion that information in a personal store is necessary to the pursuit of personal objectives that may or not be compatible with those of the organization.

One of the most common conditions in organizations is the oversupply of data to managers. This is particularly noted in functional areas where data are easy to produce, such as in finance. It is often accompanied by a shortage of reliable data and information in areas where these are difficult to produce, such as measures of effectiveness. Another form of this phenomenon is the continuance of reports that were originally generated to meet a need that has since disappeared. It may be most difficult to cancel such a report once it has become established in the organization.

A description of common disorders of the information system is similar to the contents of a textbook in physiology.[2] The fact that many conditions and disorders are described in such a text does not mean that they all exist in every human body. In the same way, not all the disorders of the information system just described exist in every organization. These disorders are, in fact, more rare in smaller organizations in which substantial mechanization of administrative and operational processes has not yet become necessary. They are more commonly found as a result of delegation of responsibility, geographic dispersion of sub-units of the organization, rapid growth and the introduction of computer support for administrative and operational systems.

Implementation – Phase I

The tasks involved in Phase I of the implementation are summarized in Table 6-1. These tasks are preliminary to the main work of implementation, but provide essential groundwork for the later activities. The tasks shown in Table 6-1 can be undertaken concurrently once the initial contact with senior management is made and the conditions under which the implementation is to take place agreed. The work is essentially investigatory, intended to establish and document the existing management pattern, the decision making processes and the information flow serving them.

A desirable first outcome of the first three tasks listed in Table 6-1 is a statement of management policy that can be endorsed by senior management and distributed for information purposes to all interested members of the organization. An example of such a statement is given in Figure 6-1. Naturally, in an actual case the statement

[2] K. J. Radford, "Some Observations on the Analogy Between Management Science and Medicine," *INFOR*, Vol. 9, No. 3, November, 1971.

Figure 6-1

COMPANY MANAGEMENT POLICY

The Company is embarking on a program of decentralization of decision making and management by objective
in which responsibility and authority will be delegated
to the level directly concerned with the activity.

Corporate management will be responsible for overall planning, formulation of standards and review of
performance. Certain services will be centralized if
this can be shown to be more economic and efficient.

Line managers will have full authority for the
management of their activities and will be expected to
account for the results of their decisions and actions.
A management information system will provide timely
data on the use of resources and success in achieving
objectives. Staff groups will provide operating management with the support required for implementation of
programs.

All levels in the Company will be expected to
manage by objective. This will involve setting of objectives at each level; these objectives and performance
towards meeting them will need to be discussed thoroughly between the various levels of management. A planning
and budgeting system will be introduced to facilitate
the whole process.

In implementing this program throughout the
Company, it is essential that:

— Programs of activity are well-defined, elimin-
  ating overlapping responsibility.
— Management responsibility is closely associated
  with each activity.
— Authority and decision making is delegated in
  keeping with the needs of managers with responsibility for programs of activity.
— Management information is organized and reported
  on an activity basis.
— Accountability for results at each level of
  management is measured in terms of degree of
  attainment of agreed objectives.

Date: President.

should contain a summary of the desires and decisions of senior management with regard to their chosen method of managing the organization rather than a repetition of the content of Figure 6-1, which is only an example. Figure 6-1 illustrates, however, the desirable characteristics of such a statement. It is short, clearly written, authoritative and signed by the President. It provides a statement of intent, without unnecessary detail and it is written in a manner that allows some freedom as to how the policy should be implemented.

Table 6-1
Tasks in Phase I of the Implementation

Meeting with senior management to ensure pre-requisites met.

Meeting with managers to explain planned program of action.

Study of management policy, objectives, activities, and pattern of decision making.

Study and documentation of existing completely specified systems.

Study and documentation of existing state of mechanization of systems, computer hardware, software, etc.

Study and documentation of existing flow of data and information to management.

The preparation of a document such as is shown in Figure 6-1 is not an easy task. The final version may contain many compromises. Ideally, it should be endorsed and accepted by all members of senior management without reservation. It is best written by a member of senior management, rather than by an information systems specialist. It should not be published until it is reasonably certain that the document and all its implications are understood by all members of senior management. Preparation and acceptance of a document of this nature may be accomplished quickly in some cases. It is wise, however to expect the process to take at least six months in average circumstances and possibly as long as nine to twelve months.

This time is well spent if close and intimate contact is established between managers and the senior information system specialists involved in the implementation. The time can be used also to study the objectives of the organization and to prepare an explicit statement of these objectives that is agreeable and acceptable to senior management. At the same time, the activities presently being undertaken in the organization can be studied and documented as a first step in establishing a program structure that is appropriate to the agreed objectives. The pattern of decision making within these activities should also be documented, to the greatest extent possible, at this stage.

While contact with managers and definition of management policy, objectives and present activities is being accomplished by one group working within the implementation team, another group can study and document the various parts of the existing information system. This work consists of discovering all completely specified systems existing, or in process of implementation, in the organization and recording in detail:

1/ The nature and source of input data.

2/ The processing specifications.

3/ The nature and recipients of output from the system.

4/ Data and information retained in the system.

5/ Data and information passed to other functions in the organization.

6/ Any existing capability for monitoring the system.

In many cases, this information exists as a result of a well-documented process of mechanization or computer support. In others, the system may have been introduced without any supporting documentation. In this case, an arduous task of creating that documentation is necessary.

As a separate project, but concurrent with the above, details of the state of mechanization of completely specified systems are documented. This involves recording the complement of data processing machines, computers and software available in the organization. This provides a base point from which future studies of computer support can start.

Development and mechanization of systems is usually an on-going process. As one project is completed, other systems appear as candidates for computer support and the complement of computer hardware and software in the organization may increase accordingly. It is best to place restrictions on the number of new applications which are started and on changes to the computer hardware and software, at least in the early months of the implementation of a new information system. There is a danger that this will be regarded as a retrogressive and unnecessarily restrictive measure by those committed to new developments. On the other hand, it is a necessary preliminary to the introduction of new techniques of mechanization and computer support should these prove desirable as the implementation proceeds.

The last task listed for Phase I of the implementation is the study and documentation of the existing flow of data and information between sub-units in the organization. This can be achieved, as far as the formal aspects of the existing information system are concerned, by listing the contents of existing reports and other periodic communications. Other useful information that can be collected is the data on which the first of a particular set of reports was initiated, the office or person initiating the report, and the use to which it is now put.

Phase I may be expected to last from a minimum of about six months in a small organization to as much as eighteen months in a large one. During that time, management policy and objectives are reviewed by senior management and resources marshalled to undertake the implementation. Considerable contact and good will should be generated between managers and the information system specialists charged with the implementation. The components of the existing information system are studied and documented and some restraint placed on development of new systems and computer support, pending decisions to be made early in Phase II. Phase I of the implementation does not come to an abrupt end as Phase II starts. There is normally some period of overlap in which both types of activity exist.

Implementation – Phase II

A summary of the tasks undertaken in Phase II is given in Table 6-2. This is the period in which the foundations of the new information system are laid. It is the period during which the greatest amount of resources is required but also that during which the first results of the effort are realized.

As with Phase I, many of the tasks outlined in Table 6-2 can proceed concurrently, although the degree of interdependence of the Phase II tasks is greater than is the case with those in Phase I.

Working from the objectives of the organization as a whole established in Phase I, the first task is to establish a program structure, according to the principles described in Chapter 2. Having accomplished this, the next step is to assign responsibility for the program categories, sub-categories and elements to what may be called *responsibility centers*. These responsibility centers may in fact be identical with the administrative sub-units shown in the existing organization chart. On the other hand, some rearrangement of responsibilities may be suggested to management during the process. For this reason, the tasks of establishing responsibility centers and of assigning program categories and elements to those centers are ones in which senior mangement must be intimately involved and for which they must take ultimate responsibility. This is the stage in the implementation at which personnel in the organization may perceive the greatest threat to their status and future. It must be conducted, therefore, with understanding and firmness and using an approach best designed to bring the greatest cooperation from managers and personnel at all levels in the organization.

Table 6-2

Tasks in Phase II of the Implementation

Establishment of the program structure and of responsibility centers.

Establishment of information system standards.

Creation of an elementary common data base.

Establishment of the historic store.

Creation of an elementary management reporting system.

Redesign, as necessary, of completely specified systems.

Study of required computer support.

The result of this process may be illustrated by a diagram such as is shown in Figure 6-2.

Level 1 in this diagram represents a responsibility center comprising the organization as a whole, under the president or head. Level 2 comprises the major responsibility centers reporting to the president and responsible for one or more major program categories. Responsibility centers at Level 3 may be responsible for program categories, for sub-categories, or for elements of programs, as may centers at any other lower levels in the organization. It is usual that there is a correspondence between the level of responsibility center and the level in the program structure for which it is responsible; but this is not necessarily so. Centers at Level 4, for example, may be responsible for activities which constitute a clearly definable and separate program category, but one which is of minor importance in the overall organization.

Responsibility accrues from the lower levels in the diagram to the

Figure 6-2
Levels of Responsibility Centers

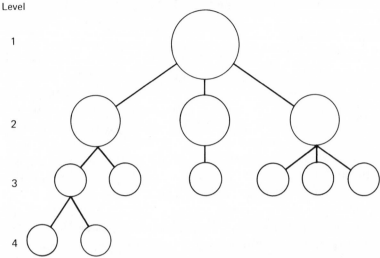

Level

1

2

3

4

upper levels. In the same way, objectives of a responsibility center at a lower level are necessarily a sub-set of those at the next higher level to which it reports. This diagram of responsibility centers is essentially an organization chart as far as it relates to the conduct of the program elements in the organization. No two centers should both be responsible for an individual program element; no program element should exist that is not assigned to a responsibility center. The process just described may involve major changes in the structure of management in the organization concerned. On the other hand, it may merely confirm a management structure that already exists.

The establishment, or confirmation, of the program structure and the responsibility centers is the first step in the creation of standards relating to the information system. The second is the definition of quantitative measures of use of resources, efficiency and effectiveness in meeting objectives which were discussed in earlier chapters. These measures ultimately become a language in which all communication in the formal information system is expressed. The second task in Phase II (noted in Table 6-2) is therefore the establishment of these standards and of those related to documentation of system specifications, establishing data formats and codes for data and information and computer support.

Many of these standards can be drawn from practices and conventions already existing in the organization. There is little point in changing established conventions which serve the present purpose well. What is necessary, however, is to decide on those items which are to be standard, to publish them as such, and to include them in a manual of standards for the organization.[3] This work is best done by a small group made up of members from those parts of the organization most concerned with the standards in question. Once a standard form has been established, all those concerned with the implementation of the information system must adhere to it, although a procedure for revision of standards, through the same mechanism as for the establishment of a standard, must be available.

Once the process of establishing standard formats for data and information has started, work can commence on the creation of the common data base. Membership of the common data base is limited to those data and pieces of information that are common to two or more administrative or operational systems or to one of these systems and the management reporting or information retrieval systems. From the descriptions of existing systems documented in Phase I, candidates for inclusion in the common data base are brought forward and after standard definitions, formats and coding are agreed upon, these items of data and information may be placed in the base. It is necessary to point out, at this stage, that membership in the common data base may not affect the *physical* location of the data or information. Membership in the base is a *logical* attribute of the item; it may be stored physically anywhere in the system. It may even be stored in more than one place in the system, such as in personnel and financial systems; but wherever it is found, it is in the same standard form.

As more and more existing systems are redesigned to conform to information system standards and specifications, as more procedures are completely specified and mechanized and as more and more use is made of the management reporting and information retrieval systems, the common data base grows. This gradual process of creating the data base is preferable in many ways to that in which a common data base is designed and introduced all at one time. It ensures that only data and information which are truly common in the organization are admitted to the base. The new data base is established with the minimum of disruption of operations. Most important of all, the piece by piece consideration of entrants to the base allows time for modifying any administrative procedures concerned with editing and updating the data and information.

---

[3]W. Hartman, H. Matthes, A. Roewe, *Management Information Systems Handbook*, McGraw-Hill, 1968, p. 8.

Concurrent with the establishment of the early versions of the common data base, arrangements should be made for setting up a historic store of its contents. At the same time, an attempt can be made to recreate, from existing records, the contents of the base as they would have been in earlier time periods. This process extends the store of historic information in standard format available to management in the early stages of the implementation.

As the work of establishing standard measures of use of resources and effectiveness proceeds, the agreed measures can be incorporated in a first version of the management reporting system. Ideally the contents of the management reporting system are decided by meeting managers' requests for information of this nature in periodic reports. In practice, this procedure is usually supplemented by a process of designing reports for managers on a trial basis and modifying them as a result of comments and criticisms received. The early versions of the management reporting system must co-exist with existing management reports in many forms and should complement these existing reports, rather than compete with them. In this way, the new and the old reports can be combined at some later date in a fashion best suited to the requirements of managers at the various levels in the organization. *It is usually best to start the new management reporting system with reports between Level 2 and Level 1.* These are less voluminous and have a relatively greater impact on the organization as a whole. Acceptance of a form of reporting at the higher levels is likely to ensure that the task of extending the system to the lower levels is more easily accomplished.

While the above work in Phase II is proceeding, a technical component of the implementation team can consider the questions of standards in data processing and the nature of the necessary computer support. This involves, in the first place, selection of computer programming languages, establishment of standards of documentation of computer-supported systems, and selection of a data, or file, management system. Once these have been established, the method of providing the necessary computer support can be investigated. This involves decisions between acquiring an on-site computer or using outside service bureau facilities for each major application, the question of renting or buying any computers to be acquired and the nature of the service, in terms of access and response time, required from the computer facilities. With these matters under active consideration, other members of the implementation team can turn to any necessary redesign of existing completely specified systems and to consideration of any other processes that should be mechanized.

This second phase of the implementation may last for a considerable time. Typical durations range from 12 to 36 months depending on the nature of the organization and the complexity of its operations and administrative procedures.

Implementation – Phase III

The third phase of the implementation, which may start 1½ to 4 years from the initiation of the project, consists mainly of the continued development of the components of the information system. As more and more administrative and operational systems are incorporated into the information system and converted to run under the chosen computer software and hardware, the amount of common data increases. Acceptance of the management reporting system as a means of formal communication between managers and its extension to all levels also tends to broaden the content of the data base. More and more systems move into routine operational status and the information system specialists concentrate on maintenance of these systems and production of improved versions. These later versions are prepared so as to fit into the modular design of the overall system, in order that introduction of improved components is achieved with minimum disruption of operations.

Table 6-3

Tasks in Phase III of the Implementation

Continued development of administrative and operational systems, management reporting system and common data base.

Creation of an information retrieval system.

Maintenance of the overall information system.

The decrease in design work in Phase III as the overall information system becomes operational makes effort available to evaluate the work done in the earlier phases. Some improvement in overall efficiency may be possible as a result of this evaluation. At this stage, effort may be available, also, to provide an information retrieval system for efficient and timely responses to requests for information from the data base and the historic store.

A summary of the implementation schedule is shown in Figure 6-3. There is no specific time at which it can be said that the

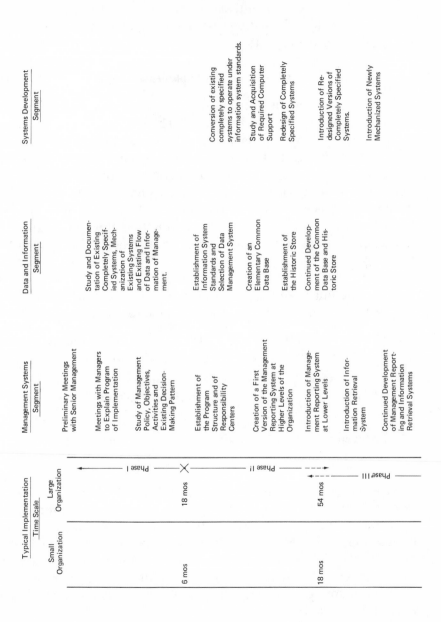

Figure 6-3

development of the system is complete. The major effort switches from development to maintenance, but continued work is required to ensure that the information system continues to meet the needs of management of the organization.

Organization for Implementation

A chart showing the organization of the teams involved in the implementation is given in Figure 6-4. The first team to be created is the committee of senior management shown at the top of the chart. This consists of most of the members of senior management of the organization and is under the chairmanship of the president or his immediate deputy. The role of this committee is to oversee the design and implementation of the system. Members of this committee should be prepared to continue this task throughout the full implementation period. Typical terms of reference of this committee are:

- To determine the objectives to be achieved and the approach to be taken in the implementation of the information system.

- To decide on priorities of design and implementation according to the resources available for the project.

- To review progress reports on the implementation and to take any necessary steps from time to time to align the work with the stated objectives.

- To evaluate the effectiveness of the information system as it comes into operation.

Participation of the most senior members of the organization is essential, because the design and implementation of an information system usually causes some review of management policies and of the responsibilities of the various components of the organization. The existence of such a committee heading the implementation stresses the commitment of senior management to the project and provides a mechanism for resolution of disagreements that may arise at lower levels in the organization.

The day-to-day work of implementation is directed by an executive subcommittee of the senior group. This consists of a small number of senior managers and the senior information systems specialist and should preferably be under the chairmanship of a manager who will be a future candidate for president of the

Figure 6-4

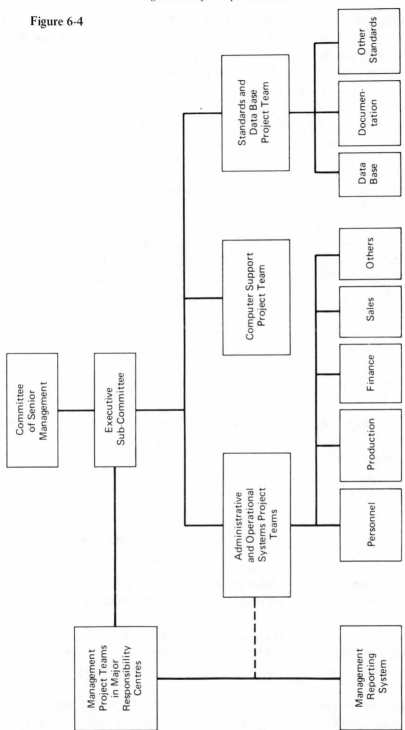

organization. In large implementations, this committee should be full time for the duration of the work. In smaller projects, it can be a part-time task for its members; but in this case, it is important that the subcommittee continue to direct the work with undiminished vigor throughout the implementation.

To the left of the chart in Figure 6-4 are shown management project teams set up in each major responsibility center to direct the implementation there. The chairman of each of these teams reports directly to the executive subcommittee to ensure coordination of the implementation within the organization as a whole. The members of these project teams should be primarily managers who will eventually use the system when it is in operation. The project teams should include also a smaller number of information system specialists. The task of these project teams is to ensure that the implementation meets the requirements of management in the individual responsibility centers. The terms of reference of such a project team should include:

- To establish objectives for the responsibility center and activities designed to attain those objectives.

- To review the management structure of the responsibility center in the light of the defined objectives and activities.

- To supervise preparation of detailed specifications for the portion of the management reporting system relating to the responsibility center.

- To supervise preparation of requirements and specifications for administrative and operational systems in the responsibility center.

- To evaluate the effectiveness of the information system as it is implemented in the responsibility center.

- To report to the officer in charge of the responsibility center at all stages of the implementation of the information system.

In the same way as with the executive subcommittee, the management project teams should be full-time if the size of the implementation warrants it, and otherwise part time, but continuing throughout the implementation.

Three technical project teams are shown in the center and right of the chart in Figure 6-4. These teams are composed primarily of information systems specialists and the head of each team reports to the executive subcommittee. Membership of these teams is full time, although particular specialists may work on more than one team. The technical teams are responsible for:

1/ Design and implementation of the administrative and operational systems.

2/ Specification and provision of computer support.

3/ Establishment of standards and the common data base.

Staff members who eventually will be responsible for the operations of these components of the information system should be members of these teams.

The existence of an organization for implementation, such as is shown in Figure 6-4, ensures that decisions can be made at the levels where the design and implementation is taking place and also should disagreements arise the problem can be passed to a higher level for resolution. The highest level of decision is the committee of senior management. The very existence of this committee may ensure that a minimum of problems are passed there for resolution.

Staffing of the Implementation Teams

The implementation teams should be made up of both managers and information systems specialists, in different proportions according to the work involved. The executive subcommittee and the project teams in the major responsibility centers should have a much greater proportion of managers than specialists. The technical project teams should be composed mainly of specialists with proportionately smaller involvement of managers. The combination of the skills of managers and specialists in any one team ensures that all aspects of the task are considered. The managers have a thorough knowledge of the operations of the organization and of their requirements for information in day-to-day decision making. The specialists usually have little detailed knowledge of operations but are skilled in modern quantitative methods and processing of data. If these two groups can work together in an atmosphere of good will, a successful implementation can be ensured.

The managers most suited for membership in the project teams are those who will be candidates for senior positions in the next ten to fifteen years. These can be found at the time of the implementation in the second level of management in the major responsibility centers. Martino has given five reasons for selection of managers in this class, which can be summarized as follows:[4]

1/ Such managers understand the day-to-day problems of the organization.

2/ They have, or can obtain, authority to make commitments.

3/ They are, as prospective senior managers, materially interested in the success and practicality of the system.

4/ By the fact of their involvement, their subordinates will actively assist in the implementation.

5/ When they return to their normal work after taking part in the implementation, they will have a significant impact on ensuring successful operation of the system which they have helped design and implement.

There may be considerable problems in securing the services of a sufficient number of these managers to serve on the project teams. By their very nature, they are filling key positions in the organization. Nevertheless, assignment of such managers to the implementation is an indication of the importance placed on the project by senior management. Their assignment provides an opportunity for their subordinates to take greater responsibility for the time period involved. This should not cause friction as long as the individuals concerned are assured of their future role in the organization.

Many organizations do not have sufficient analysts and information systems specialists within their own resources to undertake the design and implementation of a large scale system. Because a far greater effort in this technical area is needed during implementation than when the system is operational, it may not be desirable to build up a team of specialist staff members, only to see them surplus to requirements at a later date. One solution to this problem lies in the introduction of contract personnel, who are prepared to work in the organization until the design and implementation is well in hand. Contract personnel can usually be found who are already trained and who have had recent experience in a similar project in another organization. Because of the limited nature of their contractual

---

[4]R. L. Martino, "Task Force Selection and Training," Management Development Institute, Wayne, Pennsylvania, 1967, p. 2.

obligation, these contract personnel raise a minimum of suspicion, in other staff members, that they are working to create a special position for themselves in the organization. They are usually very willing to train in-house staff to take over the work when their contractual obligation comes to an end.

Contract personnel are usually able to take a somewhat more objective view of the organization than is sometimes the case with staff members. By virtue of their experience, they can provide the leadership necessary in the early stages of the project. However, care must be taken in choosing such personnel; they should have a clear record of accomplishment in this work and be prepared to remain in the organization for the time considered necessary to complete most of the design and much of the implementation. If this can be guaranteed, a mixture of contract personnel and on-staff specialists is a good solution to a shortage of this type of skill in an organization.

It is essential to a smooth process of implementation that the specialists and analysts involved regard themselves as being in the service of the managers in the organization. As agents of change in introducing modern techniques of management and data handling, the specialists may well suggest systems that are not immediately demonstrably better or more economic than those at present in use. While the management should give a fair hearing and allow ample time for demonstration of the effectiveness of the suggestions, the eventual burden of proof must rest with the specialist. The process of proof is not simple and is seldom completely unequivocal. For this reason, a periodic review of progress, undertaken jointly by the managers and specialists involved, is a most desirable part of the implementation process.

Operations

There is a natural tendency for members of the project teams, having designed a system and run it during a test period, to think it best that they continue to administer it once it is in operation "because we know the most about the system by now." It is usually true that at that stage the team members do have the greatest experience with any particular system. However, it is their role to hand functioning systems over to the managerial and operational personnel of the organization at the earliest possible time and to take the necessary time to instruct the future users in their operation. By this means, the team members can free themselves as soon as possible for other stages of the implementation.

Certain of the activities started during the implementation are required as permanent functions of the administration of the operational information system. The most important of these are:

1/ Administration of standards and the common data base.

2/ System planning and development.

3/ Computer support.

The first of these is necessarily a centralized function in the organization and is best assigned to the manager to whom the responsibility for operational supervision of the information system has been delegated. Participation of all parts of the organization in the continuing establishment of standards can be ensured by appropriate memberships in the committees devoted to this task.

The ultimate location of the continuing system planning and development and computer support activities depends on the management structure of the organization these activities must serve. As Taylor and Dean have pointed out:[5]

> In companies where the normal management structure is highly centralized, a basically centralized computer system works best. Likewise in decentralized companies, decentralized computer activities appear to work best.

The level of experience and competence in systems work and computer support activities existing in the organization is an important factor in deciding where these functions should ultimately be placed within the organization. In organizations where computer-supported systems are being introduced for the first time and where experience of the staff with these techniques in general is low, it is best to concentrate the systems design and computer support activities initially in a central group. In this way, the experience and professional competence of the specialist personnel grows faster and the opportunity to absorb and train new staff is greater. The existence of a strong central group also has many advantages in negotiations with suppliers of goods and services in the initial stages of implementation and operations. As the level of competence increases and as the general familiarity with computer-supported

[5] James W. Taylor and Neal J. Dean, "Managing to Manage the Computer," Harvard Business Review, September-October, 1966.

systems grows within the organization, the activities of the central group can be decentralized to the extent desirable to match the management structure.

It is not necessary to decentralized all aspects of system design and computer support at the same time. It is normally best to decentralize the work of systems specification and design at the earliest possible time, so that the work can be carried out in the actual part of the organization where the application exists. In the initial stages, computer programming effort and the design of computer support can be obtained from the central group. As competence and understanding of computer-supported systems grows in the organization, these activities can also be decentralized, if this is judged desirable.

This evolutionary relationship between a central group and other interested parts of the organization has a number of advantages in the development of computer-supported systems in the organization as a whole:

- It allows the orderly local growth of computer-supported systems while providing adequate service as this development takes place.

- It ensures that computer hardware is not acquired by any group until full understanding of computer-supported systems exists in that group.

- It conserves trained personnel.

The purpose of the central group must be to support the development of computing in the organization, not to restrict it. Participation by users in the decisions of the central group and cooperation between the various computer users is essential to the success of the plan.

Discussion Topics

1/ How would you ensure that senior management understand the need to commit resources over a considerable period of time to the implementation of a management information system?

2/ How can the continuing support of senior management be ensured?

3/ Why is the first step in an implementation that of documenting the existing information system? Should that documentation be done with reference to the planned future system design?

4/ One of the most important activities in implementation is the establishment of information system standards. Comment on the relationship of this activity to the establishment of a common data base.

5/ The first version of the information system should be computer supported. Give conditions under which this statement is true and conditions under which it is false.

6/ Why is it important to consider a freeze on development of individual systems during the early stages of implementation? What problems can this cause?

7

Detailed Procedures in Implementation

Detailed procedures for the design and implementation of mechanized and computer-supported systems have been described in a number of texts. Those by Rosove,[1] Blumenthal,[2] Glans, Grad, Holstein, Meyers and Schmidt[3] and Hartman, Mathes and Proeme[4] give ample guidance to those engaged in this detailed work. Our purpose in this chapter is to discuss matters relating to the overall implementation and their effect on the work of project teams assigned to individual components of the system.

[1]Perry E. Rosove, *Developing Computer-based Information Systems*, Wiley 1968, pp. 67-348.

[2]Sherman C. Blumenthal, *Management Information Systems*, Prentice-Hall, 1969, pp. 102-165.

[3]Thomas B. Glans, Burton Grad, David Holstein, William E. Meyers, Richard N. Schmidt, *Management Systems*, Holt, Rinehart and Wilson, 1968.

[4]W. Hartman, H. Matthes and A. Proeme, *Management Information Systems Handbook*, McGraw-Hill, 1968.

The Administrative and Operational Systems

There are four distinct stages in the design and implementation of a mechanized or computer-supported system:

1/ Preparation and documentation of an agreed set of specifications for the system.

2/ Determination of the machine or computer services required to operate the system.

3/ Test and introduction into operations.

4/ Evaluation of operating performance against specifications.

The preparation and documentation of an agreed set of specifications for the system is a major part of the work of implementation. These specifications must include:

- Details of data to be input into the system.

- Procedures for gathering these data from sources within and external to the organization (these are the equivalent of the *sensors* that Wiener said would keep the organization *en rapport* with the outside world[5]).

- Specification of the processing required to support the administrative or operational function.

- Description of the data and information required to monitor the operation of the system and to assess its efficiency.

- Details of the outputs required by the function.

- Specification of the data and information that must appear at the interface with other components of the information system.

- Details of a means of retaining data and information in a historic store and of the procedure to be used to decide when it can be discarded.

The work of preparing these specifications is best shared between the managers responsible for the function and the information systems specialists involved. If this is not possible, the documented version of the specifications must be agreed between all concerned,

[5] Norbert Wiener, *The Human Use of Human Beings*, Avon Books, 1967, p. 47.

the managers realizing that the system that will be produced can differ very little from that described in the specifications and the specialists understanding that they must produce a system to meet those specifications. Agreement on the specifications is essential and time taken at this stage to change and rewrite the specifications in order to ensure agreement, is time well spent. For either managers or specialists to write the specifications without reference to the other party is to risk a bad implementation.

Having reached an agreement on specifications, the next step is to assess the machine or computer support required to operate the system. This aspect of the work is dealt with in detail later in this chapter. It is at this stage that first estimates of the cost of operating the system are produced. If these costs are judged too high, there is still time to rewrite the specifications to achieve lower cost. There follows a period of machine processing design or computer programming which is of the same order of duration as the specification-writing phase. As the system programming advances, the opportunity to make changes to the specifications drops sharply. On completion of programming, the system is tested, modified as necessary to meet specifications and declared ready for operations.

In actual practice, the introduction of a new system into operation is seldom this straightforward. It is rare that the specifications that are written at the first attempt satisfy the ultimate requirements of the managers in charge of the function, despite the fact that the specifications are agreed as a step in the implementation. There is a learning process involved, of which the work on the original specifications constitutes only the first step. During this learning process, the capability of the team charged with writing the specifications develops and their familiarity with the system increases. In order that the system be implemented, however, it is necessary to set some date on which the specifications are frozen. Changes to the specifications after that date are increasingly difficult to accommodate as the programming work progresses. Freezing of the specifications does not however, and should not, stop the development of ideas among the project team members.

The best method of meeting this situation is to arrange for several versions of the system to be produced in sequence. After the specifications of the first version are frozen, most, if not all, new ideas and changes are diverted toward a second writing of the specifications, much in the same way as successive versions of the design of an aircraft are produced. System design is undertaken in a modular fashion so that later versions can be introduced with the minimum of effect external to the individual system involved. The procedure is illustrated in Figure 7-1. By this means, the results of the first machine or computer-supported version of the system can be assessed when this version reaches the operational stage and the results of this assessment can influence the specification of the second version. This process can be repeated until a version that is judged satisfactory is obtained. Changes to the specification required by changing internal and external conditions can be accommodated throughout.

It is quite rare that a satisfactory operating system is achieved in the first version. For this reason, it is unwise to plan for the existing operational system to be discarded immediately after results are obtained from the first version. Prudence calls for parallel operation of the existing system and the first, and possibly the second, version of the mechanized system. During this period of parallel operation, realistic costs of the mechanized system can be obtained and compared with costs of the present system. This comparison may itself have some effect on specifications for later versions. In extreme cases, the mechanized version may be discarded and the existing system retained.

Adoption of this process of successive versions and parallel operations undoubtedly increases the cost and the effort required in implementation. Nevertheless, this cost is often amply repaid in terms of the facility with which the new systems are introduced.

It is generally wise to allow more time for development of a computer-supported system than seems necessary at first, particularly if the application is in a new field. Systems of a type that have been in operation for some years, such as payroll and accounts receivable, have become more standard in recent years and can be implemented more quickly and with more assurance of success. Other systems, requiring the use of less well developed techniques, may need a longer period of implementation before satisfactory operation can be achieved.

It is a good policy to ensure that standard techniques of machine or computer support are used during the implementation, rather than new ideas which may be less well tested and which may turn out to be less efficient than is supposed at first. It is easier to accommodate changes in specialist personnel if standard techniques of programming, documentation and file handling are used. For the same reason, it is wise to insist on thorough documentation of the implementation, from the original specification through to a detailed record of the computer program developed. This is particularly

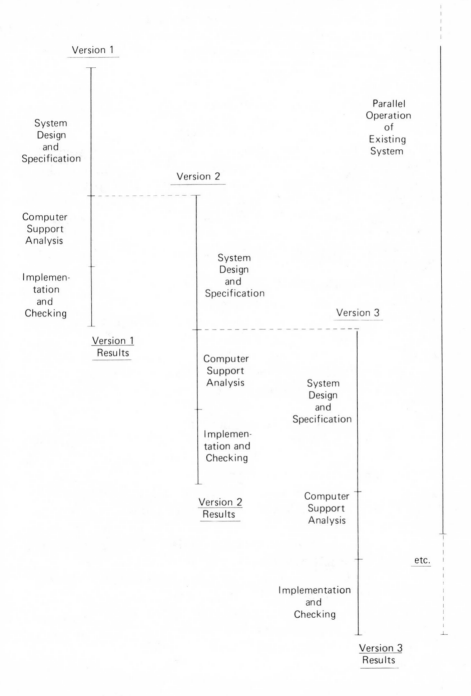

Figure 7-1

necessary where continual modification of the application is expected. Computer specialists may not include sufficient time for documentation in their original estimates of development time, and this is another reason to allow more time for implementation than appears necessary initiålly.

Data Management

Administrative and operational systems comprise, in general, a series of procedures for processing data and producing specified output. The data are stored in files; and it has been, and still is in many organizations, standard data processing practice to set up these files within the individual systems, without regard to other files containing the same data in other systems in the same organization. The semi-autonomous operation of these systems and of the functions that they serve has provided no reason to eliminate this practice.

The concept of a common data base, however, requires that data and information that are common to two or more functions in an organization be stored in standard definitions, formats and coding. As each candidate for inclusion in the common data base is discovered and put forward for admission, its definition, format and coding may therefore be changed from those used in the individual system files where it appears prior to its candidacy for admission to the data base.

In practice, it is more convenient to admit candidates to the common data base in groups related to key data elements, to which other data can be related. Such key data elements include, for example, employee number or name, customer account number, and supplier name. The key data elements form the focus of what has been called a *masterfile*.[6] Each masterfile contains a series of master records; for example, the employee masterfile includes one master record for each employee, containing all data on that employee that is judged necessary to admit to the common data base.

At the initial creation of the common data base, there are normally a number of immediately apparent candidates for entry as masterfiles. Following this initial step, other candidates present themselves for admission as the management reporting system develops and as its requirement for data and information in standard form increases. Even after several years of operation, however, the

---

[6]Adrian M. McDonough, *Centralized Systems,* Thompson Book Co., Wayne, Pa., 1969, p. 87 et seq.

common data base may contain only a small percentage of the data and information in the organization. The majority remains in the files attached to the administrative and operational systems, serving a single function only and in a format and code appropriate to that function.

The process of admitting data to the common data base does not necessarily imply that the physical location where it is stored is changed. The common data base is a conceptual entity and its members are not necessarily stored together physically. They may remain in the files attached to the administrative and operational systems where they occur and may therefore be stored in more than one place in the overall information system. By definition, however, their format and coding and the parameters to which they refer are standard throughout the system.

During the course of the implementation, there is a continual need to change the characteristics of the contents of the files attached to the various components of the information system. This is caused by continued re-evaluation of the contents of these files and by the candidacy of data elements for admission to the common data base. It is therefore undesirable that the structure of the files and the characteristics of their contents be an inseparable part of the structure of the administrative and operational systems. If this were so, any change in the file contents and their characteristics would require a redesign of the system in which the file appears.

Separation of the processing instructions from the files on which they operate can be achieved by a technique that has been called *file independence.* This method of implementing a computer-based system provides for the processing specifications to include a description of the data to be processed in logical form, which is independent of the physical structure of the data. The processing specifications are therefore separated from the files of data on which they operate. The necessary link between the logical description of the data to be processed and the file structure itself is undertaken by a data management system. Changes in the physical structure of the data can therefore be made without affecting the logical description of files in the processing specifications.

The Data Management System

File independence is introduced into the design of the administrative and operational systems at the time at which these systems are redesigned in Phase II of the implementation. Before this redesign can start, therefore, it is essential to choose a data management system as a standard for the organization. There are two possible courses of action in selecting a data management system:

1/ Design and implementation of a data management system to meet the requirements of the particular information system in question. This entails the writing of the necessary software, debugging and checking the system and putting it into operation.

2/ Acquisition of a commercially available packaged system, either from a computer manufacturer or from a company specializing in such packages.

There is an increasing tendency today, toward the use of commercially available packages. This alternative brings the following advantages:

- A package is obtained that is checked out and operational, avoiding the need for debugging and operational check-out of a locally written system.

- Packages can be be obtained that have been in operation for several months or years, so that most of the "bugs" that occur in such packages have already been found and eliminated.

- The capabilities of available packages can be checked with users who have had them in operation for some length of time.

- Commercially available packages are maintained by the firm marketing the system, thus avoiding the need to maintain a locally written system.

Buying a commercially available package has, however, the following disadvantages:

- The package may not meet all the requirements of the information system and some compromise in operational capability may generally be necessary.

- It is usually impossible to obtain sufficient information on a commercially available package to modify it to meet local requirements. Even if the necessary information were available, modification would probably be a difficult and expensive task.

- A choice of a commercially available package may commit the user to a particular brand of hardware.

The data management system is at the heart of the information system and its choice is vital to successful implementation. Money spent at this stage to obtain the best possible advice is amply justified as the implementation proceeds. If there is doubt about the final choice, the factor to which most weight should be given is the reliability of the chosen system in operation.

Storage of Data

There are a number of media on which data in the information system may be stored; core memory, magnetic disks and magnetic tape are the most familiar. These media are listed in ascending order of the average time taken to retrieve an element of data for processing in the system (access time). Access to data in core memory is very fast, while that to data on magnetic tape is relatively slow. As might be expected, the cost of storage of data in the medium increases as access time is reduced. Some typical values of access time and cost, quoted by Lefkowitz,[7] show that storage in core memory is approximately one hundred times more expensive than storage on magnetic tape and about twenty-five times more expensive than use of disk.

In order to minimize the cost of data storage, it is desirable, therefore, to choose the medium of storage in relation to the speed with which the data needs to be retrieved. There is little virtue in placing data in fast access storage if, in fact, the output for which the data is used is not required at short notice. Very few outputs from the management reporting system and even from the information retrieval system are required at extremely short notice, say in a matter of minutes. Most short notice output requirements occur in the operational systems. For example, systems designed to service reservations for use of facilities, such as airline seats and hotel rooms, often require outputs in a few seconds to satisfy a waiting customer. Use of fast access storage for such applications is justified in terms of customer service. In many other cases, outputs in the space of an hour or two is sufficient and lower cost storage can be used for the data. There is a tendency to select faster access storage in order to be sure that the data are available when they are required. Uncertainty about service breeds a demand for very fast response, even though the output is not used in the application in question for some time after it is received. If this uncertainty can be removed, if service can

[7]David Lefkovitz, *File Structures for On-line Systems*, MacMillan, 1969, p. 36.

be assured so that output from systems is given at the time when it is needed, requests for fast service tend to decrease. It is in the interests of economy in the operation of an information system to reduce to an absolute minimum the number of instances when very fast response from the system is demanded.

Redundancy of Storage

The concept of masterfiles has its greatest advantage in terms of the standardization of the definitions, formats and coding of data and information. Data and information stored in masterfiles are used in two or more systems which may refer to widely different applications. These applications may require the data and information to be extracted from the masterfiles in different forms and sequences. This extraction is undertaken by the data management system, which sets up temporary files for the application in question using the data and information stored in the masterfiles. Depending on the actual application and the nature of the masterfiles, this can involve considerable amounts of sorting of the contents of these files. This may be expensive in the computer time used to process the masterfiles.

If the sort time and the associated cost become excessive, a solution is to store the contents of the masterfiles in two or more locations, possibly with different ordering of the data and information in each location. If this is done, the standard nature of the masterfile contents is not affected, merely the physical location of the masterfile used in any one application and possibly the ordering of the contents of the masterfile. The existence of more that one physical version of a masterfile introduces data and information into the information system, which is, in one sense, *redundant*. Redundancy is not, however, necessarily uneconomical. A certain degree of redundancy may reduce the operating cost of the system, by reducing the processing time required for data management. The exact degree of redundancy of data and information required in an information system can be determined as system tests are conducted in Phase II of the implementation. Should processing time and costs be too high, introduction of a greater degree of redundancy of common, standard data and information is a desirable, economic step.

The Common Data Base

The manner in which the common data base is gradually built up has been described in the previous chapters. As has been said, this buildup must be strictly regulated. One of the most important aspects of this regulation is the creation and support of a directory to the data base that can be used throughout the organization. It is not sufficient that this directory list the names of the fields within the masterfiles together with some physical data and descriptive text about the content. It is necessary that the directory system include some sort of classification code, so that relationships between data elements can be readily discovered.

There are a number of possible approaches to the choice of a classification code in the directory. A first approach might be to attach one or more departmental codes or organizational codes to each data element. This is tempting because organizational units are easily codified; but a little reflection shows that grouping data according to an organizational key might lead back in the direction of autonomous, organizationally-oriented files.

It is possible to consider adopting a naming convention for the fields (in the manner of a Dewey decimal system[8]) to permit sorting field names in order to arrive at subject matter groupings. This has the very serious disadvantage of requiring that the user name his data element in a manner that may conflict with his departmental needs. Those concerned with developing a common data base should not, if it can be avoided, concern themselves with the user's nomenclature relating to that data. Data management systems permit the user to define his own logical files and his freedom in this respect should not be restricted. Possibly, a better choice than a naming convention would be a keyword index to the descriptive text, but this is difficult to implement. Also, because of the imprecision of natural language, it is not likely to produce meaningful groupings.

One attribute of every element in the data base is the function it serves in the management of the enterprise. A hierarchy of functions may be defined and numbered to provide a code, as shown in Figure 7-2. This shows three levels of function, but further subdivision to a fourth level, or even further, is entirely practical if this can be shown to be worthwhile to the organization under study. This functional code may be applied to each data base element and allows determination of those groups of data elements which are similar in function. This procedure does not guarantee that fields with very similar contents will be next to each other in the listing but such

---

[8] Melvil Dewey, *Decimal Classification and Relative Index*, (2 volumes) 17th edition, 1965, Forest Press Inc., Lake Placid Club, N.Y.

1 **Program Development**	.1 Secretarial and Legal	.1 Secretarial .2 Public Activities Coordination
	.2 External Relations	.1 Communications and Information .2 Legal
	.3 Corporate Planning	.1 Development of Objectives .2 Long Range Planning .3 Capital Planning .4 Systems Analysis
2 **Program** **Administration**	.1 Personnel Administration	.1 Employment .2 Wage and Salary Administration .3 Industrial Relations .4 Organization Planning & Development .5 Employee Services
	.2 Finance	.1 Financial Planning .2 Financial Relations .3 Custody of Funds .4 Credit and Collection .5 Insurance
	.3 Planning and Control	.1 Program Budgeting .2 Financial Accounting .3 Management Accounting .4 Internal Auditing .5 Operations Auditing
	.4 Administrative Support	.1 Purchasing and Stores .2 Office Services .3 Library Services .4 Information and Data Processing
3 **Operations**	.1 Plant and Facilities	.1 Utilities Design and Operation .2 Facilities Design and Spec. .3 Maintenance .4 Plant Equipment Control
	.2 Production	.1 Industrial Engineering .2 Purchasing and Procurement .3 Production Planning and Control .4 Program Production
	.3 Procurement	.1 Components .2 Services
	.4 Distribution	.1 Scheduling .2 Presentation .3 Shipping
	.5 Marketing	.1 Market Research .2 Product Development .3 Sales Planning .4 Sales Promotion .5 Advertising Planning .6 Sales Operations

Figure 7-2

fields should normally be quite close together. The system permits a number of function codes to be applied to each group of data, since any one group may serve more than one function. The effect of this is to make it more likely that similar groups of data will be listed close together and, therefore, will be noticed as candidates for consolidation into masterfiles.

One of the main advantages of this functional coding of data elements is that it leads in the direction of functional alignment of the data base. This is very desirable, *because information tends to flow more along functional than formal organizational lines*; and the common data base is, after all, a communications medium. Possibly, the most compelling advantage of functional coding over organizational coding is that it is *relatively independent of organizational changes*. The functional structure should change only if the essential nature and objectives of the enterprise itself change, rather than with each reorganization.

The insight into information handling that arises out of the functional classification of data is almost certain to give rise to organizational changes. However, like the creation of the data base, this can be evoluutionary in nature, with the impetus coming from senior and middle management, rather than from the information systems specialist.

The Process of Consolidation of Data

Consider for a moment what files are and what is to be accomplished by classification and consolidation of their components. Essentially, a file is a list of members, which are called records, each of which has two parts. The first part is the identifier and, as the name suggests, is unique within the file. The other part of each record is called the descriptor and it is a block of information applying to that particular identifier but not necessarily uniquely. The descriptor is often subdivided in hierarchical fashion, occasionally ten or more levels deep.

In attempting to classify file contents, the only physical realities involved are at the highest and lowest levels. The entire physical record and its physical properties are real and absolute. Similarly, the individual field, or named unit of data which includes no other named units of data, has real objective qualities, even though its name may be variable.

Data groups at intermediate levels may be given names and may be assigned some of the attributes of fields, but they have no physical reality in the file. Although it is certainly useful to document their existence to help the user and to give insight into the use to which the file is put, intermediate data groups do not bear on the question of commonality of data.

Every physical file has at least one field which contains an identifier, which is unique in the file and which is called a keyfield. It is possible to create files in which this is not the case, but such files are invariably files of transactions which are sorted on a particular field and then matched to this field in a masterfile which is then updated, effectively consolidating records with identical fields. The dictionary or directory system must identify these keyfields. A listing of keyfields is a listing of all of the entities which have attributes recorded in the data base. This listing contains as many items as there are files in the data base, but it is to be expected that the list contain duplication of keyfield content and, more notably, of type of entities. For example, a number of keyfields may be expected to appear with labels like employee name, employee number, payroll number, social insurance number, all referring to employees of the organization. Clearly, all such files are candidates for consolidation into a masterfile about employees.

As the files are consolidated, it is not necessary that all duplication be eliminated immediately. In fact, this is probably inadvisable. The various files relating to employees, for example, may have been consolidated with certain immediate gains in efficiency, such as the elmination of duplication of such non-contentious items as date of birth, marital status, seniority, employment history and job history. In many cases, however, there are fields which appear to contain the same data but which need to remain distinct by virtue of lack of agreement between users as to the physical characteristics of the field or some aspect of the contents. It is the proper function of the information systems specialist to point out that there are, for example, five fields in the personnel file called 'annual salary.' He should not, however, attempt to force standardization on the five or more users of those fields. Nevertheless, he might quite properly ask that the sources of the data for these various fields be identified unequivocally, leaving the resolution of the problem of standardization to the managers concerned.

These managers are those who controlled the autonomous files under the previous organization of the data and who had power of decision over access to the data. Once the data are transferred to the common data base, this power of decision must be replaced by rules governing the right of access to the data which are agreed between all users. This is especially important in the case of confidential data such as personnel records and sales performance. In the same way, information on the same subject occurring in more than one autonomous file may previously have been updated at different times, possibly with data from different sources. With the standardization of these data, the person or office responsible for updating the common data must be established. In accepting responsibility for updating part of the data, a department must again abide by rules established and agreed by all users of the data in question.

Transfer of data from existing autonomous files to a common data base, therefore, requires changes to be made in the administrative arrangements necessary to provide access to the data and to update it. These changes are best approached gradually and progressively, in step with the evolution of management responsibility. A single massive conversion might bring chaos to the administration of the data on which the operations of the organization depend. It might also result in a rejection of the common data base by managers and the consequent retention of personal hoards of data, in opposition to the common data base principle.

As the process of consolidation proceeds, the use of statistics that can be recorded in the directory system may suggest certain areas of the data base that are candidates for special treatment. Certain functional data groups may merit on-line query or on-line update. In many of these cases, ordinary hierarchical file structures will continue to suffice. In certain other areas, however, the use of more sophisticated and costly network file structures might be justified. A major advantage of the evolutionary approach to the creation of a common data base is that decisions of this nature can be deferred until a great deal of experience has been gained of the nature and content of the data base and of the demands on it in the day-to-day operations of the organization.

What has been described here has not been the creation of a data base, so much as the discernment of one. It is, perhaps, a little like the approach that the Eskimo is said to take toward carving a walrus from a piece of stone. He first visualizes a walrus embedded in the stone and then simply chisels away all that does not look like a walrus.

The Management Reporting System

The starting point of the implementation of the management reporting system is the series of reports that are produced regularly and periodically in the organization. These are listed in Phase I of the implementation and they remain in existence as long as they are found necessary. If they are produced by separate parts of the organization, it is a good idea to gather them into a composite management report, without at first changing their form or content.

Such a composite report is a good subject of conversation when approaching managers to determine their needs for information. The implementation team can say, "Here is a composite of all the reports that are available to you. Please tell us where they are deficient, what information you need in addition, and what information can be omitted." The objective of such an approach to managers is to determine the information they need to fulfill their decision-making tasks. It is sometimes difficult, however, to determine the exact pattern of decision making in an organization. Managers are sometimes at a loss to define the information they need in their day-to-day work. To quote Daniel:

> Seldom is the open approach of asking an executive what information he requires successful. For one thing, he may find it difficult to be articulate because the organization structure of his company is not clearly defined. Further, and more important, there is a widespread tendency among operating executives to think of information exclusively in terms of their companies' accounting systems and the reports thus generated.[9]

The situation is further complicated by the fact that management information must be passed between subordinate and superior as a necessary complement to the delegation of responsibility. The information that needs to be passed depends upon agreements made at the time that the responsibility is delegated. In many cases, such agreements are not explicit with regard to the actual information exchange required.

The best approach in these circumstances is for the project team in a responsibility center to propose a format for management reports from the second to the highest level in that center. Having checked the format with the managers concerned, reports are then produced periodically and circulated alongside the composite of existing management reports. Much of the data in the new format may be taken directly from the existing reports. Some new data and information can be added; and as the process of defining standard

---

[9] D. Ronald Daniel, "Management Information Crisis,' *Harvard Business Review*, September-October 1961, pp. 91-101.

measures of efficiency and effectiveness advances, these new parameters are shown in the new management reporting system as well.

For an initial period of as long as one or two years in some cases, the new system is produced alongside the existing reports. Ample opportunity is given for managers to criticize the new format and to suggest additions or deletions. In the initial stages of the parallel production of new and old format, the official formal reporting system remains the old format. At some time, however, when sufficient time for development, change and adaptation of the new format has elapsed, a decision by senior management that the new format is the official formal reporting system for the organization is announced. Data and information in the old format continues to be produced for as long as this is useful. Management makes it clear, however, that, effective some convenient date, the new management reporting system is the formal communication vehicle in the organization. The new format continues to be developed after the changeover, as necessary to meet the needs of the organization. Once the new system is accepted at the high levels, compatible systems are developed serving the lower levels. The existence and acceptance of the new system at the higher levels makes the task of implementation throughout the organization easier.

The amount of information reported in all cases is the smallest quantity which meets the requirements of the managers concerned. This policy may meet with some opposition from those who feel more secure when surrounded by large amounts of data. Whereas the wishes of managers for information should be respected as far as possible, clear cases of oversupply or overdemand for information must be raised by the information system designer as contrary to efficiency in overall system implementation.

The Information Retrieval System

In contrast to the management reporting system, the information retrieval system is allowed to grow by demand. Because the requirements of managers for information to meet needs that do not occur regularly cannot be estimated, it is best to await recognition by managers that a store of data and information is available that may be helpful to them. Circulation of a summary of the contents of the store and of procedures for retrieval of the data and information increases the awareness of users of its existence.

Many users of the information retrieval system are not aware of the relationship between retrieval time and the cost of the service. This is illustrated in Figure 7-3.

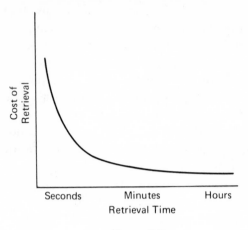

Figure 7-3

Cost of very fast retrieval (in a matter of seconds) of data and information from a computer-based store is very great compared with retrieval of the same material in a few hours. There are some circumstances where fast retrieval is necessary. There are others, however, where supply of the data and information in a few hours (or overnight) would meet the user's needs and be significantly less costly to the organization as a whole. In the initial stages of the design and implementation of the information retrieval system, therefore, users are requested to consider their needs for access to the store very carefully and to demand fast access only where it is absolutely necessary. In some cases, this approach is reinforced by introducing a penalty or cost for fast access that the user is prepared to pay if his demand for this service is absolutely necessary.

Computer Support

There are three distinct stages in the design and implementation of a computer-based information system:

1/ Preparation of detailed specifications for the components of the system that are to be computer supported.

2/ Choice of a data management system and other data processing standards.

3/ Specification of the computer services and machine devices necessary to service these systems.

It is most desirable that these steps be undertaken in the order shown. It is practically impossible to specify accurately the computer services needed to operate a system that has not yet been described in detail. Unfortunately, many organizations take the opposite approach[10], characterized by, "let's get a computer in and we will build the system around it." In this, they sometimes are misled by computer manufacturers who are anxious to sell hardware and who make promises of performance in terms that are very difficult to enforce once the hardware is in place. Computer specialists in the organization itself, who see the acquisition of hardware as a factor aiding their own progress and status, often contribute to the reversal of the logical order of implementation.

Once the design of systems has reached the stage where an estimate can be made of the required computer support, the information system designer is faced with three questions:

1/ Whether to install and maintain a computer system in-house or to take service from an outside facility?

2/ If the decision is to install an in-house computer, should the equipment be purchased or rented?

3/ If the decision is to use an outside facility, what are the important considerations in negotiating for these services?

An In-House Computer Versus Outside Services

The rapid increase in the number and variety of computer service bureaus in the last few years has introduced an alternative to the installation and maintenance of an in-house computer. Assuming, for the moment, that an outside facility provides exactly the same service, at the same cost as would an in-house computer, use of the outside facility offers the following advantages:

1/ The number of operational computer personnel required in the organization is greatly reduced.

2/ A smaller number of computer software personnel is required because the system software is maintained at the outside installation.

3/ It is generally easier to obtain increasing amounts of computer

---

[10] James M. McKeever, "Building a Computer-based MIS," *Journal of Systems Management,* Vol. 20, No. 9, September 1969.

power as requirements increase without either acquiring a larger computer than necessary at first or changing the installation at a later time.

4/ Service can be obtained immediately from an installation that is operational, thus avoiding the disruption of the shakedown period of a new facility.

There are, however, two important conditions attached to the use of an outside computer facility. It must provide the required *access*, so that the computer services are available when required, and it must provide the same *security* and *confidentiality* of data and information as could be guaranteed in an in-house installation. Provided that these two conditions are met, and assuming the outside facility offers the required services, the decision between use of the outside facility and installation of an in-house computer rests on the relative costs of the services.

The costs of operating a computer facility fall into three categories: rental (or amortized capital cost) of hardware, operating expenses, and systems and applications planning. In a study of 33 major installations,[11] the average proportions of costs in these three categories were 37%, 39% and 24% respectively. The normal rental agreement for computer hardware calls for a minimum payment of one shift rental and for substantially less for operation in excess of one shift in any month. The average cost per time unit of computer service is shown on the upper lines in Figure 7-4. This may be compared with the lower line showing the average cost per time unit of computer service for a fully utilized, rented computer. The broken line represents similar information for a purchased computer, but the actual position of this curve depends on the manner and period of amortization of the purchase cost. Costs of hardware and operating are therefore considerably higher if an in-house computer is utilized for only a small proportion of the available time. The question now arises as to whether these costs are lower or higher than the costs of comparable service from an outside facility.

This comparison must be made in each individual case, taking into account the particular circumstances surrounding the application. In general, however, if a service bureau operates the same equipment as the in-house user and gathers work from other sources to increase utilization, the average cost per unit of computer service from the

[11] James W. Taylor and Neal J. Dean, "Managing to Manage the Computer," *Harvard Business Review*, September-October, 1966, p. 19.

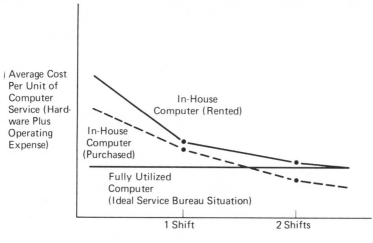

Figure 7-4

bureau should be less (taking into account hardware and operating costs only). The smaller number of personnel required by the user also adds to the advantage of the service bureau. Unfortunately, the comparison is seldom that simple. Service bureaus generally have larger computers, more sophisticated and more varied software, sales staffs and other characteristics that increase overhead. The only course in practice is to make a detailed cost comparison for the particular circumstances, after having ensured that the services offered, the access and the security of data and information are satisfactory.

There are two circumstances when use of a service bureau is generally recommended. When computer services are first introduced into an organization, or when the applications envisaged are relatively small, there is usually little economic advantage in installing in-house equipment. It is often a good approach to start operations using a service bureau, taking care to design the system so as not to become dependent on the bureau facilities; and to plan to make a decision with regard to an in-house computer at a later stage when more experience is gained with the applications. A more accurate estimate of the cost of using the service bureau will be available at that time. The same approach can be adopted in the case of an organization that operates a computer facility that appears to be overloaded or outdated. In these circumstances, new applications, and such existing applications as are suitable, can be placed on a service bureau and the decision to reequip or use a service bureau for all computer work can be made at a later time when more reliable data are available.

The Decision to Rent or Buy an In-house Computer

If the decision has been made to acquire in-house equipment, the choice remains between renting or buying the computer. The factors involved in this decision may be summarized as follows:

Equipment should be bought if the applications involved are long-term (longer than the average three to four years economic break-even time between renting and buying) and if the applications are likely to be stable and not to expand beyond the capacity of the equipment within the break-even time. Examples of such applications are those in which computers are used to control manufacturing processes and those applications involving services to stable or predictable populations; for example, servicing of government sponsored social security programs.

Equipment should be rented if the number of applications in the organization is likely to expand rapidly or if the scope of any of these applications is likely to expand.

The history of computer applications to date is one of very rapid expansion once the use of such equipment is accepted. Unless the future can be seen very clearly, therefore, it is advisable to rent rather than buy. In cases of doubt, it is normally possible to obtain a purchase option, whereby a proportion of rental charges already paid can be put toward the cost, should purchase appear to be desirable at some later date.

Use of Outside Computer Facilities

One of the most important considerations in the use of an outside computer facility is the method by which users communicate with the remote computer. This can be accomplished by a conventional delivery service or by installing direct communication links between the user and the remote computer. Both methods of delivery of data and processing instructions may involve extra costs, which must be taken into account in the cost comparisons mentioned earlier.

Remote connection to a central computer has many advantages in terms of convenience to the user. The direct communication to the central facility gives the feeling of contact with the computer which is important to many users. There is a relationship between the amount of data passed to and from the computer and the time required for delivery of these data, which is illustrated in Figure 7-5.

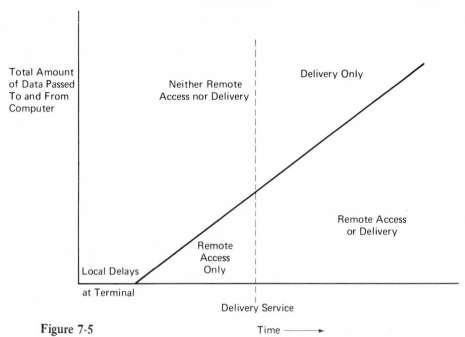

Total Amount
of Data Passed
To and From
Computer

Neither Remote
Access nor Delivery

Delivery Only

Remote Access
or Delivery

Remote
Access
Only

Local Delays

at Terminal

Delivery Service

Figure 7-5

Time ⟶

The sloped line represents the capability of a communication link to pass data. Since the capacity, in terms of characters passed per second, of such a link is constant; the slope of the line is constant representing, for example, a certain number of characters per second. The greater the capacity of the link, the higher the slope of the line from the horizontal axis. The possibilities of delay in passing data through the terminal equipment in the user's office (for example, if the terminal is in use on another job) is shown by drawing the sloped line intersecting the horizontal axis some distance from the origin.

The significance of the sloped line is that all combinations of amounts of data and delivery times, represented by a point on the diagram, that fall below it are possible with a communications link of capacity represented by this line. Above the line are points representing situations in which the amount of data could not be delivered by the communications link in the time available. The dotted vertical line represents the time taken by a conventional delivery service to transport data to the computer and to return it after processing. This might be perhaps two hours for a truck in a busy city or possibly thirty minutes for a hand messenger between close locations.

The sloped and dotted lines divide the diagram into four spaces. Combinations of amounts of data and required delivery times that fall into the lower left space are possible only by the use of the remote access communications link. The delivery service would be too slow. In the upper right space, only the delivery service can provide the necessary passage of data; there is too much data to be passed over the communications link in the time available. In the lower right space, both methods are possible; and in the upper left, neither. A diagram of this nature provides an insight into the desirability of remote access techniques in any application. Many administrative and operational applications in which users require fast delivery of small amounts of data fall into the lower left space where remote access is a good solution. Large data processing tasks for which delivery in a few hours will suffice may fall into the upper right space and be adequately supported by a delivery service.

Analysis of requirements for remote access suggests many variations on the ideas expressed in Figure 7-5. For example, large amounts of data can be sent by conventional delivery service and only essential commands transmitted by the communications link. However, this may reduce the convenience of the remote access operation. Another possibility is to store data and instructions at the central computer in a readily available form (such as on magnetic disk) rather than pass it over the communication link on each occasion. In this case, storage costs must be assessed and considered in overall cost comparisons.

Security of the System

The information system occupies a unique and vital position in an organization, by virtue of the data and information that it contains and the functions in the organization that it serves. Loss of any part of the system may affect the necessary activities of acquisition, use, retention and transmission of data and information. Providing for the physical security of the system against accident, inquisitiveness or direct attack is, therefore, a most important aspect of implementation. Loss of part of the information contained in the system may be even more damaging, especially if the loss results in an advantage to a competitor. Another important aspect of implementation is, therefore, providing for confidentiality of certain classes of data and information in the system. As with any other system in an organization, there is the possibility that a staff member or a member of the public will take advantage of expert knowledge to engage in fraud by manipulation of data or information in the system. A number of cases of accident, attack, inquisitiveness, theft of data and fraud have already been reported.[12]

Simple security measures can give good protection against theft and willful damage to components of the information system. These include strict control of access to processing facilities and data storage and rigorous screening of those personnel who are allowed access to these facilities and data. Protection against accident includes measures to minimize or prevent damage due to fire, flood, power failure and civil disorder. Special measures are necessary to protect data and information in the system and to provide an opportunity to reconstruct such data and information from historic stores located in areas geographically separate from the normal operational area, should the operational system be disabled or destroyed.

Stealing of data and information or fraudulent tampering with the system are much more difficult to prevent because the guilty person often exercises considerable ingenuity. Such persons usually operate alone. The most reliable method of preventing fraud is the installation of an independent system of checking and auditing all transactions.

The following guidelines for the protection of data and information in the systems are based partially on those quoted by Chu[12] :

- Current files should never be released for processing without the existence of a back-up file.

- Back-up files should be under the control of a group separate from the computer operation's group and should be stored in a separate location.

- Computer programs should be rigorously tested before introduction into operation and should be supported by back-up copies.

- Computer programs that might be changed for the purposes of fraud should be checked at random intervals against their back-up copy.

- Input data should be checked by independent editing processes, as a measure against fraud.

- Spot checks on operations should be made at random times in

[12] Albert L. C. Chu, "The Corporate Achilles Heel," *Business Automation*, February 1, 1971.

computer-based systems, by use of independently installed checks and audits.

Security and confidentiality is of prime concern in the use of an outside computer service bureau, particularly if remote access by telephone line is involved. Special measures are necessary to ensure that the data and information passed to and from the remote computer is not lost, stolen or tampered with. These measures may involve private communication links, scrambling devices to make data and information unintelligible and physical security at the computer site. In some cases, considerations of security and confidentiality of data may forbid use of a remote computer not under the administrative control of the organization.

Discussion Topics

1/ Production of successive versions of computerized systems may increase the cost of implementing such systems. Do the advantages of this method of approach outweigh the extra cost? Is there a better approach?

2/ What groups of data in a typical organization are first candidates for inclusion in masterfiles?

3/ What are the advantages of specifying file structures independently of the system design in implementing a computer based system?

4/ What is the relationship between the characteristics of the physical unit used for storage of a data set and its use in the information system?

5/ Is redundancy in storage of data undesirable? Are there conditions when redundancy is, in fact, desirable?

6/ Discuss the available methods of indexing data sets in the common data base. Which one would you choose and why?

7/ A common data base should be built up gradually, in full cooperation with the personnel using the data. True, false, or maybe, and why?

8/ Is asking an executive what information he requires the best way to determine the content of the first version of the management reporting system? What problems arise in this method of approach?

9/ Which levels in the organization should be the first to have a management reporting system designed for them?

10/ In what circumstances should use of a computer service bureau be considered and in what circumstances should a bureau not be used?

11/ Under what circumstances should remote access link to a computer be employed? What are the alternatives?

12/ What steps should you take to ensure the physical security of your information system?

8

The Impact of Implementation on the Organization

The implementation of an information system such as has been described in previous chapters is unlike the implementation of a routine data processing application. Such an application affects only a part of the organization and is concerned only with minor decision-making processes. *The information system described touches on vital functions throughout the whole organization and is intimately linked to all decision-making processes in the organization.* The work of implementation requires examination of the structure of management, responsiblity for activities, and the pattern of decision-making. In some cases, even the goals and objectives of the organization may be revised as a result of work which is a necessary preliminary to the implementation.

The implementation and acceptance in operation of an information system of the type proposed requires the existence in the organization of what Argyris has called a "climate of rationality."[1]

---

[1]Chris Argyris, "Management Information Systems: The Challenge to Rationality and Emotionality," *Management Science*, Vol. 17, No. 6, February, 1971, pp. B275-292.

Rationality in this context is related to the definition proposed by Eilon[2] that was discussed in Chapter 3, but is somewhat broader. Eilon's definition provides a useful means of defining completely specified decision processes. Rationality in the sense described by Argyris embraces a logical step-by-step approach to the problems of management, which avoids emotionality and may inhibit the growth of effective inter-personal relationships.

The Impact on Management

The implementation of an information system can have a significant effect on the manner in which managers approach their decision-making tasks. The required climate of rationality implies a greater reliance in making decisions on quantitative factors and completely specified processes. Managerial influence in these processes is elevated from the trivial resolution stage to the more complex activities of problem formulation and selecting criteria for decision making. More emphasis is placed on logical and rational solutions to problems and less on judgment unsupported by facts.

This change of emphasis may not be received gladly by managers in the organization. The increased reliance on quantitative factors may cause them to feel restricted, or to feel they have less room to maneuver. When communication is more in terms of well-defined and understood parameters, the exchange of information is increased and there is less room for equivocation in discussions after the initial communication has taken place. This may cause managers to withdraw from communication for fear of being committed. This is particularly noticeable in those who are not confident of their position or their ability or who have not established a relationship of trust with their superiors.

The process of implementation may reveal behavior, policies, practices and standards that have been accepted and used by mutual arrangement between members of small groups, but which, nevertheless, are to some extent in conflict with the rational statements of objectives and activities produced for the organization. Activities contributing to personal, rather than organizational, objectives may be revealed. As Argyris states;[1]

"Equally important . . . is that, as the informal is made more explicit, it comes under the control of management. The result

[1]Chris Argyris, "Management Information Systems: The Challenge to Rationality and Emotionality," *Management Science,* Vol. 17, No. 6, February, 1971, pp. B275-292.

[2]Samuel Eilon, "What is a Decision," *Management Science,* Vol. 16, No. 4, December, 1969, p. B174.

may be that the participants will feel increasingly hemmed in . . . . These feelings in turn, can lead to increasing feelings of helplessness and decreasing feelings of self-responsibility resulting in increasing tendency to withdraw . . . . ."

The information system tends to make more understandable information available to more people. There is less opportunity for managers to withhold information in order to increase their power within the organization or their impact on important decisions. The greater availability of meaningful information reduces the influence of executives who had previously exercised authority on the basis of incomplete or invalid information.

The emphasis on delegation to the computer of completely specified decision-making processes may be regarded as threatening by staff members who have specialized in such a process as a means of ensuring security of tenure of their job. Such personnel may work long hours and overtime in an endeavor to convince superiors, and possibly themselves, that they are indispensable to the organization. A suggestion that the process be automated may be opposed on the grounds that considerable judgment is involved. The real reason for opposition is often a defense of established security of tenure in the organization. Suggestions that judgmental ability be applied instead to higher levels in the decision-making process, such as selection of criteria for resolution, may be opposed because the staff members involved are unsure of their ability at the higher level of activity.

The climate of rationality and the increased use of quantitative data and information leads to less opportunity for ambiguity. A manager's success in the past ". . . may have come from selecting an admittedly ambiguous course of action, but with resources and power, making it come to reality . . . . If a decision was successful, he could point to where his influence was important. With optimal ambiguity and fluidity, he could also reduce the probability of being convicted of incompetence if the decision was not successful."[1] Implementation of the information system is in some ways similar to requiring the manager to play nomination pool (where the pocket and the particular ball to be sunk in the pocket are stated before the shot) rather than the normal game in which credit for skill and foresight can be claimed from a lucky shot.

The emphasis in the information system on measures of effectiveness and efficiency may cause managers to feel that their perfor-

[1]Chris Argyris, "Management Information Systems: The Challenge to Rationality and Emotionality," *Management Science*, Vol. 17, No. 6, February, 1971, pp. B275-292.

mance is being assessed entirely on the basis of these quantitative parameters. This should not be the case. Furthermore, goals and objectives should be discussed and agreed beforehand, during the budgeting process and to the greatest extent possible, the achievement of these goals should be regarded as a joint endeavor between superior and subordinate. Nevertheless, when quantitative factors assume a greater importance in assessing the work of staff members, they may well feel in times of adversity that they are "being judged by a number." In these circumstances, the manager may begin to suffer the frustrations that employees in production processes have experienced in the past as a result of the work of industrial and quality control engineers who designed their work and monitored their performance.[1]

Greater use of measures of effectiveness and efficiency may be feared by employees who are incompetent or who may feel that they are incompetent. These employees have a stake in anarchy and can be expected to resist the introduction of any system that might reveal their true or believed incompetence. Furthermore, such employees may have turned to participation in *intra-* and *inter-*group politics as a means of masking their incompetence. The more rational climate tends to reduce the impact of such politics on the management of the organization.

To summarize, the introduction of an information system requires managers to exercise new skills at a level higher than may have been the case in the past. Some managers may perceive the move as a threat to their position, status and careers. They may react by showing an uncooperative and hostile attitude toward the implementation. This is more likely to occur among the less competent and among those who fear that they do not possess the competence to meet the challenge of the new managerial techniques. Those who are engaged in covert, personal activities or who feel that the examination of management structure and techniques that precedes the implementation may reveal unpalatable features of their past record of performance, may also resist the introduction of the new system.

This resistance is most often found in older organizations that have become ineffective over the years. The very lack of effectiveness in such organizations may be a major factor in the decision to review management techniques and redesign the flow of management information. As an organization slowly disintegrates, inter-personal

[1]Chris Argyris, "Management Information Systems: The Challenge to Rationality and Emotionality," *Management Science,* Vol. 17, No. 6, February, 1971, pp. B275-292.

cooperation decreases and groups tend to concentrate on survival and the continuance of the jobs of members of the groups. Some groups turn to activities that they do well, but which have little relation to the objectives of the organization as a whole. By engaging in such activities, these groups may hasten the deterioration of the organization by their consumption of scarce resources.[3] The proposal to implement an information system in such an organization may be interpreted as a direct threat to the survival of groups of this kind.

In a younger organization, staff members are often well motivated and informal communication between them is good. In these circumstances, the need for a formal information system may not be recognized. Just as budgeting seems unnecessary when money is in good supply, a specially designed information system may not be regarded as important when the organization is thriving. Nevertheless, the introduction of an information system early in the life of an organization can be one factor in maintaining its momentum and resisting the process of deterioration.

The Information Systems Specialists

The information systems specialists concerned in the implementation are distinguished from the managers in the organization by their knowledge of automatic data processing and possibly some training and education in management and organization theory. These are relatively recent areas of specialization; for example, formal courses in computer science have been taught in most North American universities for little more than a decade. When these courses were first introduced, the emphasis was on scientific computing rather than on business data processing. This latter was introduced into the curricula of universities and technical colleges at a much later time. The rapid development of computer science and technology has rendered much of what was taught ten years ago out of date and introduced subjects, particularly in the area of computer software, that are of very recent origin. The result is that very few senior managerial personnel received formal instruction in modern computer science in their undergraduate years or even had much contact with computers in the pursuit of scientific or engineering studies. To specialize in computer systems is essentially a young man's profession. Those older persons involved have obtained their knowledge

---

[3]K. J. Radford, "Some Observations in the Analogy Between Management Science and Medicine," *INFOR*, Vol. 9, No. 3, November, 1971, p. 245.

and experience by working in the field, by taking short courses or, in a small proportion of cases, by returning to full time education after some years work experience. Much the same may be said of those engaged in the practice of the related techniques of management science.

The first general applications of digital computers were in science and engineering. These involved numerical solution of mathematics and engineering problems that were not amenable to a completely analytical approach and for which numerical solution without the aid of computers was beyond the practical capability of teams of human beings. The design of the early computers available for general use reflected the requirements of these applications. In fact, as late as 1953, the view was held by a substantial portion of the computer community that the digital computer would not be used in business applications and that the number of large computers required in the United States would be very small. When data processing computers were introduced into business in the late 1950's and early 1960's, their role was almost exclusively to undertake the calculations previously assigned to business machines. The applications reflected the computer's capability to handle large volumes of simple numeric calculations quickly. Because the greatest number of such calculations in a business organization occurred typically in the area of finance, the computer was introduced first to service these applications. In many cases, the computer, and the computer specialists who operated and tended the machines, were placed under the administrative control of the financial component of the organization. Usually, the introduction of the computer did not change the administrative and functional procedures in the areas where it was employed. Its primary role was to expedite the handling of the increasing volume of financial transactions more efficiently than could be the case using manual procedures or the existing business machines. As computers grew more powerful and as their capability to produce output increased, the newly introduced machines multiplied the amount of data that was processed, primarily because the capability to do just that was available. Printers capable of writing a thousand lines a minute were soon producing reports so voluminous as to be beyond the capability and endurance of executives to read them.

The concentration by managers on financial reports was therefore increased by the greatly increased capabilities to produce these reports. Meanwhile, some other parts of the organization turned to the use of computers. They were introduced into control of production processes. Models of operations produced by the application of the methods of operations research required computer support. Managers in functional areas, other than finance, began to seek computer aid in processing administrative data.

These developments provided ample work for the relatively small number of computer specialists. A mystique surrounded the computer. Many senior managers were persuded to invest large sums in computer installations and services on the assumption that it was necessary to maintain pace with the competition. This was often done without sound knowledge of the usefulness and limitations of the computer in business applications. Managers were encouraged in this course by computer suppliers and often by their own computer specialists. Most of those engaged in the application of computers were genuinely convinced that their work would provide significant benefits for the organization. A minority saw the opportunity to further their careers and raise their status in the organization. The shortage of qualified computer personnel aided those who sought high positions and salaries comparatively early in their careers.

Relationships Between Managers and Computer Specialists

To many managers who have spent ten or twenty years building up their operation, the introduction of a computer appears as a threat to their authority from a source that they do not have the knowledge and experience to comprehend. In some cases, a bitter confrontation arises between the managers and the computer specialists. To the managers, the specialists appear young, inexperienced in the "real" world, brash, confident and enjoying support from senior management that they themselves would have appreciated in their long years of work in the organization. Frequently, a recently introduced computer specialist earns a salary similar to that which the manager had taken many years to achieve. To the computer specialists, the managers often appear slow, uncomprehending, hemmed in by constraints and unappreciative of the advantages that the computer could bring.

An analysis of the difficulties experienced in relationships between the two groups has been made by Hebden.[4] The fact that Hebden refers to the computer specialist group by the somewhat outmoded term "EDP Department" and that this article was published as late as

[4] J. E. Hebden, "The Importance of Organizational Variables in the Computerization of Management Information Systems,' *Journal of Management Studies*, May, 1971, pp. 179-198.

May 1971 is probably evidence of the later application of computers to business problems in the United Kingdom. Nevertheless his article describes situations which still persist. For example:

> While a management team that is opposed to EDP may seek to implement its opposition by furthering the 'distance' between itself and the EDP staff, it will, by thus furthering the distance, ensure that many of its most gloomy prognostications regarding EDP are fulfilled. Senior management, it has been suggested, may further this distance by controlling the size of the department and the level of sophistication at which the installation may operate. Distance at this level facilitates the maintenance of distance at the level of implementation — the level of middle management.

Argyris has conducted a study of the operations of a team acting as information systems specialists in a large corporation.[1] He states:

> Although the group had been given a generous budget and excellent facilities, top management's receptivity to quantitative analytical thinking had left much to be desired. Several reasons may be offered. First, as mentioned above, the executives had succeeded because they had the capacity to make choices, based upon intuitive heuristic understanding. Once a decision had been made, they were experts at marshalling human and financial resources to implement the decisions. They were skilled at making their decisions "come true"; they were skilled at turning a decision into a self-fulfilling prophecy.
>
> Second, the organization had developed quantitative financial analyses which were used to manage the corporation. These financial systems which seemed to the (specialist) team, to be inadequate, antiquated and tied to reporting history, were buttressed by a powerful organization that had influence with the top management.
>
> Finally, the state of the art in management science information systems is still primitive compared to the demands of the management.

Argyris found that the information systems specialists lost some of their composure under stress during the implementation, produced

[1]Chris Argyris, "Management Information Systems: The Challenge to Rationality and Emotionality," *Management Science,* Vol. 17, No. 6, February, 1971, pp. B275-292.

more behavior evaluated in the study as conformity or as antagon-ism, suppressed their feelings of tension by intellectualizing and did little to help their fellows to become more open, explore new issues or take risks. He found also that the senior managers involved acted in the same way. In fact, both information systems specialists and managers reacted to stress in a way that inhibited effective inter-personal relations and, therefore, problem solving.

Some Methods of Dealing with These problems

Methods of dealing with problems in human relations arising during the implementation have as their aim the elimination or reduction of the elements of conflict and threat between the two major groups involved—managers on the one hand and information systems specialists on the other. A first approach (which has already been advocated in Chapter 6) is to form teams to undertake the major tasks in the implementation which include both managers and specialists. This has the advantages of breaking down to some extent any barriers between the two groups and of building up the degree of interpersonal relationships between members of the teams. It involves some difficulties for those in a minority in any one team, who may feel that they are being asked to work out of their natural environment, or to act as "Judas goats" (used to lead animals to slaughter) in the process of conversion of their colleagues.

Some problems may arise by the miscasting of computer systems specialists in the role of information systems specialists. Many computer specialists have little experience outside the design and implementation of computer supported, completely specified deci-sion processes. These, as we have seen, are an important part of the information system. They do involve, however, decision processes to which a completely rational approach has already been largely accepted by the managers concerned. Many other parts of the information system cannot be approached in the same rational manner. To do so, is to risk rejection of the whole concept of the information system.

Computer systems specialists cannot be regarded as information systems specialists until they have had experience in dealing with those decision-making processes that are not completely specifiable. These are the areas in which the manager is skilled and in which he applies his experience and judgment. *In fact, it is usually more practical to train managers in the fundamentals of information processing (at least to the point where they can direct the work) than it is to provide computer specialists with the experience and judgment necessary to deal with the higher level decision processes.* As Dearden remarks:[5]

> Indeed, I believe it is much more practical to teach the new information technology to the function experts than to teach information technologists functional specialties. After all, the man who could master all the functional specialties—the true MIS expert—would have to be an intellectual superman. . ."

A good strategy is, therefore, to select members of management who are to be team leaders in the implementation and to provide them with sufficient training and experience in computer based systems that they may discuss these subjects without disadvantage with those whose specialty is in this area. The managers themselves, then, become those responsible for the implementation. The senior information systems specialist for the duration of the project may, in fact, be a manager seconded for the task. Computer systems specialists take on a support role of providing detailed technical assistance in the implementation of a plan devised and directed by the managers themselves.

Once the team leaders are trained, they can take part in a series of seminars aranged for managers at all levels in the organization with the purpose of:

1/ Explaining the management philosophy adopted by senior management.

2/ Describing the process of implementation of the information system and the proposed schedule.

3/ Explaining the management techniques and tools that will be designed into the new system.

It is important that managers from the organization itself provide the greatest proportion of the presentations in these seminars. By this means, senior members of the organization are seen by participants to be actively involved in the implementation. The members making presentations will learn quickly by virtue of having to present material to their colleagues.

[5] John Dearden, "MIS is a Mirage," *Harvard Business Review*, January-February, 1972, p. 94.

One of the aspects of the implementation of greatest interest to the participants in the seminars, is the schedule of implementation. Unfortunately, in the early stages this is not easy to define precisely, particularly because the speed of implementation depends to some extent on the rate of acceptance of the system by the managers themselves. Participants at the seminars should be warned against expecting too precipitate a change in their day-to-day work. On the other hand, if in the six months following the seminar, there are no signs of progress, some degree of cynicism may result. It is desirable, therefore, to institute a program of updating the information that the participants receive at the seminar and to assure them, during the original seminars, that some follow-up is planned. This follow-up can take the form of a periodic information bulletin or of half-day follow-up meetings, possible at six monthly intervals, at which some of the speakers at the original seminar report on progress to date. All these sessions should be designed to explain a course of action decided by senior management that will change the manner of management reporting in the organization. They should, of course, be integrated with the normal training program of the organization. They should in no circumstances replace it.

All the methods of dealing with the human aspects of the implementation just discussed are to some extent based on the assumption that the problems that arise can be resolved rationally. To quote Argyris once again:[1,6]

> Education and structural rearrangements assume that people will respond rationally to the new stimuli these learnings and changes create. This assumption is valid up to the point where people begin to threaten each other and are in conflict. Then both sides regress and respond ineffectively. Rational solutions may delay the moment of conflict, but they do not get at the underlying problem, namely, no one has been able to program human activity significantly to eliminate or reduce conflict and threat. Moreover, in the cases where it has been attempted, the "success" has been due to the fact that the protagonists got the message and suppressed the expression of conflict in front of top management. This does *not* mean that rational solutions such as education and

---

[1]Chris Argyris, "Management Information Systems: The Challenge to Rationality and Emotionality," *Management Science,* Vol. 17, No. 6, February, 1971, pp. B275-292.

[6]Chris Argyris, "Interpersonal Barriers to Decision Making," *Harvard Business Review*, March-April, 1966, pp. 84-97.

structural changes will never work. The strategy being suggested is that the competence of *both* managers and MIS professionals in dealing with emotionality and strain in interpersonal and inter-group problems must be raised. As their interpersonal competence in these areas increases they will naturally turn to education and structural changes. We would predict, on the basis of other research, that their commitment to education and the changes will then be internal, not merely external (imposed).

Discussion Topics

1/ How is the climate of rationality required for implementation of an information system related to the concept of rationality in decision making?

2/ Are the frequently noticed reactions of managers against implementation of an information system justified? How can the effect of these reactions be minimized?

3/ Can some types of organization operate without a climate of rationality? If so, which types?

4/ It is easier to teach a manager information processing than a computer specialist management. True or false and why?

5/ A computer specialist is not necessarily an information systems specialist. True or false?

6/ Is it generally true that more resistance to implementation of an information system will be found in older organizations?

9

Costs and Benefits

The subject of costs is the one to which the least attention is given in most treatments of the design and development of information systems. This is not due to lack of recognition of the importance of this aspect of the subject, but more because the subject is difficult to treat other than generally. The whole essence of a cost analysis is its relevance to a particular situation in which an individual or organization has a special interest. Other people's cost analyses are mildly interesting, but they do not have the immediate impact of a study relating to cost in one's own area of responsibility. In these circumstances, therefore, there is little alternative here but to review the sources of cost in the development and operation of an information system, to point out how expenditures should be recognized and managed and to suggest how they may be reduced by appropriate attention to details of the design and implementation of an information system.

In the first instance, it is clear that the existing information system in every organization involves certain costs which are being budgeted and paid, perhaps implicity, at the time the implementation starts. The costs of the informal component of the existing information system consists primarily of the cost of time taken by staff members in conversations, meetings and conferences. This is a necessary part of the work of these staff members and its cost is difficult to estimate; nor is it desirable that an exact estimate be attempted, in case the investigatory work required inhibit informal communication in the organization.

The operating costs of the formal component of the existing information system are more easily listed. They consist of costs of:

1/ Clerical work involved in gathering data from inside and outside the organization.

2/ Data from outside the organization obtained in hard copy or machine-readable form.

3/ Operation and supervision of business machines and computers.

4/ Planning, programming and maintenance of computer supported systems.

5/ Clerical work involved in preparation and distribution of management reports.

These costs may be a small but significant percentage of the total budget of the organization. Their total represents a figure that the operating cost of the new information system may reach without becoming an additional charge on the organization. One goal of the information system designer should be to keep the operating cost of the new system within this existing total and, if possible, to effect some savings in operating cost when the new system is installed. For this reason, it is important that the cost of the existing formal information system be established early in Phase I of the implementation, so that it can be used as a reference point in later discussions of cost.

Development Costs

The costs of the new information system may be divided into development costs and operating costs. Costs of development of a new information system arise from:

1/ The time spent by managers and information systems specialists on the design and implementation.

2/ Acquisition of any necessary computer software and data management system.

3/ Computer time used in testing new or converted programs.

4/ Acquisition of any necessary data processing machines or computer hardware.

Items 2 and 4 above may appear as monthly rental charges, which are transferable to operating cost once the system is installed. In fact, the whole development cost may be amortized by charging appropriate amounts to future operating costs if this is desirable in the circumstances facing an organization.

The amount of time spent by managers and information systems specialists varies during the implementation, both in total amount and relatively between the two classes of people. This is illustrated in Figure 9-1. At the start of the implementation and during Phase I, the total effort is comparatively small and the relative contributions by managers and specialists are roughly the same. As Phase II starts and as conversion of existing machine or computer-based systems is undertaken, the total effort increases substantially and the contribution of information systems specialists relative to managers also increases markedly. At a later stage, the total effort in the implementation decreases and toward the end of Phase III, tends to become merged with operating costs. The time period during which the implementation takes place can be lengthened if this is desirable; it is much more difficult and may be dangerous to attempt to

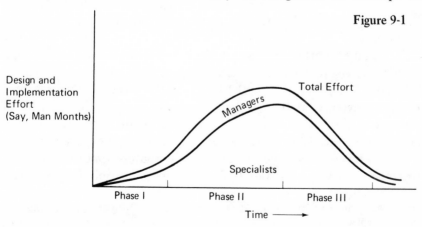

Figure 9-1

shorten it. The effect of such a lengthening would be to reduce the cost during any one financial period and probably to increase somewhat the total cost of design and implementation.

In most organizations, it is best that the cost of design and development of the new information system be budgeted and paid for from a central account. A different approach is recommended with respect to operating costs and this will be discussed later in this chapter. Central administration of development funds facilitates the early stages of design and implementation because it places control of funds alongside the initiative for introduction of the new system. It also assists in the development of standards in the organization, since these, also, must be administered centrally.

Operating Costs

The major proportion of the operating costs of the new information system are associated with the administrative and operational systems. These systems support functions and operations within the organization and their costs are an integral part of the costs of these functions and operations. Funds to meet these costs are best budgeted and administered by the managers responsible for the individual functions and operations. Once the systems have been converted to operate under standard machine and computer support techniques (in Phases II and III) they are therefore handed over to the managers to administer as part of their normal responsibilities. Some financial support from the central fund may be necessary at the outset, if costs of the converted systems are substantially higher. However, the knowledge that financial responsibility for the systems will ultimately fall to the individual managers reduces, to some extent at least, the natural tendency to request administrative and functional systems that are more elaborate and sophisticated than is necessary.

In a study reported in 1966[1], Taylor and Dean found that the cost of computer supported administrative and operational systems in 33 U.S. companies ranged from 0.13% to 1.33% of their annual revenue, with the average at 0.54%. These costs include machine rental or equivalent, operating costs and systems maintenance. Companies judged in the study to have highest effectiveness spent an average of 1.0% of revenue on operating these computer-supported systems, while those with lowest rated effectiveness spent only 0.23% in this

---

[1] James W. Taylor and Neal J. Dean, "Managing to Manage the Computer," *Harvard Business Review,* September-October, 1966.

area. These figures give only an indication of the likely operating costs of computer-supported administrative and operational systems in any organization. They do however provide a basis for initial planning, which can be updated as a result of experience as the implementation proceeds.

Whereas the costs just discussed are best budgeted and administered by the manager in charge of the individual function or operation, the much smaller total cost of the other components of the information system which serve the whole organization (the mangement reporting, information retrieval and data management systems and the common data base) can be assumed by a central unit.

Methods of Reducing the Cost of
the Information System

The computer supported administrative and operational systems should, ideally, provide more economical operation than alternative manual or other procedures. A cost comparison is a necessary part of the feasibility study preceding the introduction of these computer-supported systems. Relative costs are monitored during implementation to check the original estimates and to make any necessary modifications. Unfortunately, in many cases, costing is inaccurate. Enthusiasm for computer support often leads to underestimating its costs. It is quite rare that a feasibility study states that the introduction of a computer will increase costs significantly.

In practice, however, the introduction of computer support very often increases costs. It is not that computer support of the original procedures is necessarily more costly, but that the level of service provided is often significantly increased when computer support is available. Accounts are updated daily rather than monthly; more information is provided to customers. A computer-supported system may eventually provide much better service, but at a cost greater than the original manual system. In order to check this escalation of cost, it is necessary to monitor system implementation continually, to ensure that only necessary processing is included. Furthermore, if any increase in service is introduced, this should be subject to the same examination of benefits as the original proposal to provide computer support. An attitude of "the computer is there, we might as well use it" is almost certain to increase costs, without necessarily bringing an attendant increase in efficiency.

There are a number of other steps that can be taken during the design and implementation of the system which will result in a reduction of costs. For example, the response of the system to demands for information should be no quicker than is necessary to meet the reasonable demands of management. Quick response involves more expensive storage of data and more immediate availability of computer services. There are many situations in the direction of operations where quick response is necessary. In many others, and especially in planning and policy making, a slower response, possibly overnight is just as good and considerably cheaper.

In some cases, components of an organization may exist in geographically separated locations, each maintaining its own common data base. Communications between these data bases to update and edit common data and information should be conducted after prime business hours to the greatest extent possible, so that the cost of these communications can be kept to a minimum.

Another area in which operating costs can be saved is the elimination of unneeded and unused reports. Many reports are created to satisfy an immediate need that fades after a while. However, the request for the report is not cancelled and the cost of producing it remains. A regular check of the use to which reports in the system are put and cancellation of those no longer needed can often produce substantial savings.

Benefits

The question most often asked of the information systems specialist by the manager is, "Why should I take the time and spend the money to design and implement an information system?" This is a question that deserves serious and lengthy consideration.

Perhaps the best immediate answer is that an information system already exists in the organization. The existing system may have grown haphazardly in the past by meeting requirements totalling much more than those necessary in the environment in which the organization operates today.

Examination of the existing information system and implementation of any modifications found necessary is a step toward rationality in an increasingly rational world. The process of design and implementation can result in:

- A clearer appreciation by managers of the objectives of the organization.

- A closer relationship between the activities of the organization, and of its sub-units, and its objectives.

- A greater appreciation by management of progress made toward achieving those objectives.

- An ability to relate progress towards objectives to the resources used, or required, to achieve this progress.

- A greater ability to compare the contribution of different sub-units of the organization towards the same objective.

- Increased communication between sub-units working toward the same objective, by virtue of the standardization of terms, definitions and data formats.

- More timely and more pertinent information being available to managers to assist in their day to day tasks of decision making.

- Delegation of those decision-making tasks that can be considered to be routine to computer-supported systems, thus relieving managers of this routine work.

- Discarding unneeded data and information flow and thereby confining the amount of data and information presented to managers to what they themselves find useful in their day-to-day work.

- A greater amount of historic data being available in readily identifiable form for use in planning and other related activities.

One of the greatest benefits to a large organization resulting from the implementation of an information system such as has been described here is the increased degree of standardization of data and information in common use. A pioneer company in the implementation of information systems has found that ". . . the key to MIS is an integrated data base."[2] This increased standardization represents a partial return to the more complete sharing of data and information that exists in smaller organizations, which was noted earlier in this book as a feature of the operation of the one-man store. As a vice-president of a large organization expressed it, "Before we had the information system, we spent 80% of each meeting deciding what was the valid information. Each man had his own version. Now at least we start with a set of common information and most of our

[2]Terrance Hanold, "An Executive View of MIS," *Datamation*, November, 1972.

discussion is about the *interpretation* of that information relative to our decision problems."

These benefits are not achieved easily and the implementation of the information system may cause considerable change and disruption in the organization. The impact on personnel has already been discussed in Chapter 8. The process of changing relative priorities of production of data and information from emphasis on financial control to considerations of efficiency and effectiveness may be very difficult, especially if the financial function is represented by a powerful sub-unit in the organization. Before embarking on the implementation, therefore, senior management should at least have the assurance that they will receive periodic evaluation of progress and of the effectiveness of the information system that they have authorized.

Evaluation of Information Systems

Ideally, an information system should be evaluated in terms of benefits and costs. This may not be easy and there is no record in the literature of success in this area. As Kriebel says in a recent article,[3] "The milestone called 'evaluation' is the most conspicuous and the weakest stage in this process today." It is, therefore, an area in which we should concentrate our efforts.

An attack on this problem can be divided into two parts, the first of which relates to the completely specified systems serving the administrative and operational functions of the organization. The second concerns all other components of the information system taken together, which serve the interfunctional decision processes in the middle and upper levels of the organization.

In a well designed information system, the completely specified systems (shown as a series of circles in the lower part of Figure 5-1 of Chapter 5) represent a major portion of the operating cost. They are also the part of the information system for which assessments of costs and benefits are easier to obtain. In the earlier days of computer-supported business systems, the emphasis in evaluation was on the efficiency of the computer system, and of one computer system relative to another, rather than on the increase of efficiency of the *application* resulting from the introduction of computer support. A survey of system performance evaluation published in

---

[3]Charles H. Kriebel, "The Evaluation of Management Information Systems," *IAG Journal*, Volume 4, No. 1, 1971, p. 12.

1967[4] deals almost entirely with evaluation of computer systems. There has been very little published since then dealing constructively with the assessment of the efficiency of computer-supported *applications*

This is best achieved by insistence on cost and benefit reports throughout the implementation of a computer-supported system. These reports provide a means of evaluating the profitability of the new system as compared with that which it is replacing. An initial statement of objectives of the introduction or change of computer support is also a useful reference point as the implementation proceeds.

Cost reports should include statements or estimates of development and/or set-up costs and increases or reductions in operating costs with the new system. An estimate of performance of the new system as compared with the old in terms of quantitative measures linked to the objectives of the introduction of the new system should be recorded alongside the cost estimates. Both sets of estimates should be revised and updated during the implementation. Care should be taken that the estimates provided by the implementation team remain objective and are not influenced by the natural enthusiasm of the team for the project in which they are engaged.

As noted earlier in this chapter, the onus for evaluating the costs and benefits of the introduction of computer support for administrative and operational systems should rest with the individual managers in charge of these functions. Computer support should come to be regarded as another, admittedly more costly, form of office service available to the manager to increase the efficiency of his operation. Too often in the past, the glamor and mystique surrounding computers, the feeling of a need to appear modern and up to date, and the enthusiasm of the computer specialists for their trade have combined to preclude an objective evaluation of the use of computers in administrative and operational roles.

An evaluation of the effectiveness of the remaining part of the overall information system is much more difficult. This is the part comprising the common data base and other components that support decision making in the middle and upper levels of an organization; a part that is less costly than the completely specified systems, but which, nonetheless, is closer to the vital functioning of the organization as a whole.

---

[4]P. Calingaert, "System Performance Evaluation: Survey and Appraisal," *Communications of the ACM,* January 1967, p. 12.

The difficulty in evaluating the effectiveness of this part of the information system lies in the fact that the use of information in decision making by middle and upper level managers is not well understood at the present time. This class of decision making is predominantly personalistic, (in the sense described in Chapter 3; and some of it may be irrational when viewed against the stated objectives of the organization. Any attempt to evaluate the effectiveness of this second part of an information system must start with measurements of the use of information by decision makers and the effect of this use of information on the outcome in the decision processes in question.

This is clearly an area in which future research and investigations must be concentrated. Until a more quantitative form of evaluation is possible, assessment of the benefits must be drawn from the honestly expressed opinions of the managers in the organization and the use that they make of this part of the information system in their day-to-day work.

Discussion Topics

1/ Suppose you are the president of a medium to large organization. Why would you wish to embark on the implementation of an information system?

2/ Suppose now that you are a middle-manager in the same organization. Would your reaction to the implementation be the same, and would you see the same benefits as the president?

3/ How would you control the costs of the implementation from both positions?

4/ Many of the benefits said to result from the implementation of an information system seem to be intangible. How would you reply to this statement if placed in position of defending the decision to implement a system? Can any of the seemingly intangible benefits be quantified?

5/ Do you agree with placing responsibility for costs of the administrative and operational systems (which are part of the information system) with the managers in charge of the respective functions?

6/ Is it realistic to use the cost of the pre-implementation information system as a first target for the cost of the new system?

10

Case History

The case history of implementation of a management information system described in this chapter is a composite of experience in this work in a municipal government, a chain of hotels and a broadcasting organization. In order to present a cohesive description of the various stages of design and implementation, all experience has been brought together into the context of a fictitious broadcasting organization located in Canada. In fact, various parts of the narrative are drawn from one or other of the contributing case histories and the author is grateful for permission to use the material in this account.

The Nationwide Broadcasting Company

The Nationwide Broadcasting Company (NWBC) operates television and radio stations from coast to coast. It has studios and production facilities in eight major cities, from which programs are distributed to transmitting stations across the country. Other programs are bought from distributors. The company employs just under 5000 persons and has an annual revenue of about one hundred million dollars.

The company is licensed to operate under laws and regulations which require that it should contribute to the general objectives governing use of publicly owned and regulated broadcast frequencies, some of these being:

- To extend and develop broadcasting service to all parts of the country.

- To provide a broadcasting service in English and French serving the special needs of geographic regions and actively contributing to the flow and exchange of cultural and regional information and entertainment.

- To provide a balanced service of information, enlightenment and entertainment for people of different ages, interests and tastes covering the whole range of programming in fair proportion.

- To contribute to the development of national unity and to provide for a continuing expression of Canadian identity.

The licensing authority also requires radio and television broadcasting stations to provide programming of high quality. Nationwide's task is to operate under the above conditions and at the same time to provide a satisfactory return on investment for its shareholders.

At the time of the decision to implement an information system, the company had been in existence for sixteen years. It had grown rapidly from a modest start in radio broadcasting. In recent years, television outlets had been acquired in major cities. Management practices had centered around the objective of providing a satisfactory return on investment; and the activities and edicts of the licensing authority had had little effect to date on its operation. Recently, however, more and more pressure had been put on the company to provide a greater proportion of programs in both radio and television of a type which did not attract maximum audiences. The regulations of the licensing authority therefore acted increasingly as constraints on the achievement of the company's main objective of providing a satisfactory return on investment.

The formal information flow in the company was predominantly financial. Strict budgetary control was placed on operations at all levels. Moreover, the finance department had built up a strong organizational structure, ostensibly to provide service to managers in the various sub-units of the company, but, in fact, exercising a strong degree of control over decision making throughout the organization.

The company had been very successful in the early days and had attracted capable personnel. Many of the original personnel had risen to the senior levels of management as a result of their early contributions to the company. These senior managers were still relatively young and, with ten to fifteen years of working life still ahead of them, could be expected to hold their positions for some time to come.

The president of Nationwide was aware of the increasing demands of the licensing authority for information about the activities of the company. He sensed an uneasy feeling among senior managers that financial control was too strict and somewhat limiting to creative ability, and he noted a small but continuing decrease in the return on investment. This awareness led him to appoint one of his senior managers to investigate management practices in the company and the possible implementation of an information system.

The senior manager chosen was relieved of all other duties for the period of the investigation. He met immediately with other senior managers of the company and explained that with an initial staff of three persons he was embarking on what he described as Phase I of the work assigned to him. He said he needed the cooperation of all levels of management. The initial work would consist of an assessment of present objectives, activities, information flow and data processing in the company. It was arranged that he would report to the committee of senior management monthly on his progress in the investigation. It was also decided that a senior manager would be designated in each of the two major divisions of the company (the English and French Service Divisions) to provide liasion and cooperation with the overall company effort. These divisional officers later formed task groups of their own to direct effort in their respective responsibility centers. At the start, two managers and one senior information systems consultant were designated to work full time on the project. These were joined after three months by two information systems specialists drawn from the existing company staff. About eight other persons worked on the project a small percentage of their time at this stage.

Phase I of the Implementation

As a first step in the implementation, the senior manager on the project sought a statement of company management policy. A draft was prepared, discussed in the committee of senior managers, modified, discussed again and finally approved for distribution (see Figure 6-1). This process took place over a period of six months.

Concurrently, the small implementation group at the head office of the company studied desirable objectives for the organization in relation to its function under the existing laws and regulations. After considerable discussion of successive drafts, the set of objectives shown in Table 10-1 was adopted for the company.

Objective number 1 (return on investment) was regarded as the prime objective. Objectives numbers 2 and 3 (extension of service and maximum popular appeal of programs) provide support for this prime objective. The remaining objectives (numbers 4 to 7) are to some degree in conflict with the first three and may be regarded as constraints on the fulfillment of these prime objectives. Objectives 4 to 7 are, however, necessary to the company by virtue of the requirements placed on it by the licensing authority. The group doing this work found that there were no covert objectives in the sense outlined in Chapter 2. However, the priorities placed on the fulfillment of each of the individual objectives was regarded as confidential company information and different interpretations were given by company officials to meet different situations.

The statement of company objectives was completed and accepted by senior management five months from the start of the project.

Table 10-1
Objectives of the Nationwide Broadcasting Company

1/ To earn a return on investment satisfactory to the shareholders (after appropriate funds have been reserved for future ventures).

2/ To extend the radio and television services of the company to all parts of the country where a need and a market for these services exists.

3/ To produce and broadcast programs with maximum popular appeal.

4/ To provide programs of high standard, appealing to people of different ages, interests and tastes.

5/ To provide a suitable proportion of programs providing an expression of national identity.

6/ To provide programs with a balance between information, enlightenment and entertainment, serving the needs of different interest groups in fair proportion.

7/ To contribute to a flow of cultural and regional information, reflecting the character, attitudes and social fabric of the various parts of the country to one another.

The Existing Information System

While the work of studying management policy and objectives was proceeding, other members of the team began a study of the existing information system in the company. Completely specified systems with computer or machine support were found in: 1) payroll, 2) accounts receivable, 3) accounts payable, and 4) general accounting and costing. Systems handled manually which appeared to be completely specifiable and possible candidates for computer support were found in: 1) personnel records, 2) facilities scheduling (e.g. studios and equipment), 3) scheduling of broadcast programs, 4) audience and market research, 5) inventory systems, and 6) automatic switching of programs at the transmitter sites. Documentation of the specifications of these systems was incomplete, even for those presently with computer support. Computer programs had been patched in some cases to accommodate changes in the specifications, without an accompanying amendment of the documentation. In many cases, the operation of the systems depended on the memory and experience of one or two key personnel without whom very little could be accomplished.

As a first step in the study of these systems, the functional personnel responsible for the computer supported applications were asked to document their present systems. The results were then compared with the related computer program documentation. After considerable discussion, agreement was reached on a set of specifications that described each existing system. In each case, however, the functional managers had requirements for modifications to these systems to meet changes in conditions internal or external to the company; for example, the payroll system needed to be modified periodically to meet changes in tax deduction regulations. A procedure was devised, whereby documentation was prepared for all such proposed changes in advance of modification of the computer programs. Once the programs had been modified and placed in operation, the system documentation was formally amended. By agreement between the implementation team and the functional managers responsible for the systems, the number of modifications requested was kept to a minimum during this stage of the work. This policy was not popular with the functional managers, who felt naturally that their work was of prime importance to the company. However, prior explanation of the need for such a policy to the committee of senior management was found to be helpful in resolving disagreements during the course of the work.

Managers in charge of systems which appeared to be future candidates for computer support were encouraged to undertake a similar process of documentation. However, the policy was adopted throughout the company that computer support would not be extended to any such systems until a later stage, Phase III, of the implementation. There were similar complaints about this policy, which were resolved to some extent by contact with senior management.

The complement of computers in the company consisted of three small, second generation data processing machines, one each at the head office and two major production centers. These were all of the same basic model; but because they had always operated independently, the configurations had been modified as time went on to meet local work load conditions. At the start of the implementation, therefore, the three computing facilities were different and essentially incompatible. One contained magnetic tape drives, one magnetic disc drives only, and the third relied on card input and output. The memory sizes on all three computers were different. Consequently, in practice, an application developed for one computer facility could not be run on another without considerable modification. Cooperation between the staffs of the facilities was nominal only. Each facility had made and submitted plans for replacing the existing equipment with more powerful and more sophisticated computers. In each case, the computer facilities were under the administrative control of the local financial units, who were also the major users. The combined operating budget of the three computer facilities was of the order of $600,000 per year. This did not include, however, the cost of associated clerical work in the company, which was estimated as an additional two million dollars.

Another team member, meanwhile, documented the flow of management information in the existing system. This was done by cataloging all regularly produced internal reports and by requesting managers to list all information obtained regularly from outside sources. This process was begun at the topmost level of the company and continued by working down the organization as time went on. This seemingly formidable procedure was accomplished relatively quickly, perhaps because the bulk of the regular internal reports was financial by nature and originated in the same function within the company. An attempt was made to assess the usefulness of the existing regular reports by asking each manager the use to which he put the information contained and to whom he communicated the results of decisions based on the content of the reports. In this way, a "map" of decision-making processess within the company was built up which was of use during the construction of the management reporting system at a later stage in the implementation.

Assessment of Progress at the End of Phase I

Toward the end of Phase I, after ten months elapsed time, an assessment of progress was made for the committee of senior management. The nature of the existing information system was described to the committee and a plan for proceeding with the implementation of a modified system discussed. Details of the steps involved and the sequence of implementation in a second phase were placed before the committee. During discussion, the estimated annual cost of the existing system was noted as $2,600,000, and it was agreed that this should be an outside limit for the operating cost of the development information system.

The costs of Phase I were presented to the committee as shown in Figure 10-1, and a budget of $450,000 was shown to cover development costs in Phase II of the project in the next twelve-month period.

Phase II of the Implementation

Phase II of the implementation was planned to include:

- Design of a program structure in the company.

- Establishment of information system standards.

- Creation of a first version of a common data base

- Establishment of a first version of a historic store of data.

- Creation of a new management reporting system.

- Redesign, as necessary, of the completely specified systems.

- Introduction of necessary computer support.

In order to carry out this work, the team of information systems specialists was expanded from two to eight. The number of managers engaged full time was increased from two to four, two in the head office and one in each of the English and French Service Divisions. Part-time involvement of managers was increased significantly. In addition, some 300 staff members spent one week at a seminar designed to familiarize them with all aspects of the implementation.

Figure 10-1

**Progress and Development Costs in Phase I
of the Implementation**

Start		*Approximate effort for each item**	
		Man months	*cost ($)*
5	Statement of objectives written and accepted	3	10,000
6	Statement of management policy published	1	4,000
8	Documentation of existing computer hardware and software	2	5,000
10	Documentation of existing management information flow	4	9,000
12	Specifications of existing systems documented	27	60,000
Elapsed Time (months)			
	Total Effort Phase I	37	$88,000

*The costs in these columns relate to full time effort in the implementation in excess of that provided for the normal operations of the company. They cover development effort by managers and information systems specialists that could be specifically related to the project. Where a staff member was seconded to the project for a significant time, his salary and other costs were included. Part-time work undertaken along with normal duties was not included.

The Pr∮gram Structure

A small committee of three members, one from head office and one each from the English and French Services, was convened to draft a *pr∮gram structure* related to the agreed statement of objectives of the company. (In dealing with the pr∮gram structure, the convention was adopted of spelling the work "pr∮gram" with an oblique through the o, in order to distinguish it from a broadcast program.) This committee produced a draft pr∮gram structure and this was modified many times before adoption by the committee of senior management. The final version is shown in Table 10-2.

This structure recognized the existing separations between, English and French language broadcasting, radio and television, and program production and distribution. "Corporate Management" was introduced as a pr∮gram category to include work done, mainly at head office, that could not be identified exactly with any one of the other categories. This had as pr∮gram elements: planning, policies and standards, evaluation of performance, local head office services, and central services in the company. Each of the other pr∮gram categories had a corresponding sub-category called "Administration" concerned with similar activities within those operational categories.

Sub-categories, "Program Production" and "Distribution," were created referring to each operational pr∮gram category, (English radio and TV, French radio and TV), and these sub-categories were broken down into elements and sub-elements (in the case of Program Production). It was recognized at this stage that a further breakdown might be necessary later in the project.

Allocation of Responsibility for Pr∮gram Elements

Following adoption of the pr∮gram structure, senior management considered the present organization structure in relation to it. As a result of these considerations, the existing organization chart of the company showing a head office and two operating divisions (French and English Services) was confirmed. Furthermore, the organization of radio, television and administration responsibility centers was recommended to the divisions. The matter of organization at lower levels was left for further consideration.

Establishment of Information System Standards

A group of three, one each from head office and the two operating divisions was set up to oversee the creation of information system

Table 10-2
The Program Structure

Program Categories	English Radio, English TV	French Radio, French TV	Administration	Corporate Management
Sub Categories	Program Production	Distribution		
Program Elements	Information Entertainment	Broadcast Transmission | Program Sales	Program and Production Planning Operations Management Evaluation Central Services	Planning Policies and Standards Evaluation Central Services Head Office Local Services
Sub Elements	News and Current Affairs Music Arts, Letters and Science Variety and Light Entertainment Drama Sports and Recreation Feature Films			

standards in the company. This group had the right to co-opt other members as necessary in the consideration of a particular subject or area. It was the only group in the company with the power to create standards for the information system; and, as such, it published and updated from time to time a standards manual. The major areas of activity of the group were:

- Procedures in system development and documentation.

- Establishment of quantitative measures of resources and effectiveness in the pursuit of objectives.

- Descriptions of masterfiles contained in the common data base.

- Data formats and coding in the information system.

In addition to the above, the group was given the responsibility of administering the prøgram structure, once this had been established within the company.

Certain areas were designated which were not considered to be under the aegis of the standards group; for example:

- Actual targets and goals to be achieved during a budgetary period.

- Measurements of efficiency and other work standards.

- Policies governing operational and functional areas.

- Organization within responsibility centers.

These matters were considered to be the prerogative of company managers in the course of their day-to-day work.

The group recognized that sufficient flexibility must be maintained at all times to allow standards to be modified if this was found to be necessary in the development of management techniques and policies in the company. The goal of the standards group was to serve, rather than restrict, the purposes of management.

When the need for any particular information system standard arose within the company, the situation was brought before the standards group, where agreement was sought on the details of the standard. After approval by the group, the standard was considered established and it was entered in the standards manual. Recommendations for changes in existing standards were handled in the same way. In the event of disagreement, the matter was passed to the committee of senior management for resolution.

In the course of Phase II of the implementation, over an elapsed time of some two years, the following standards were established by the group:

1/ *Project Memorandum.* The project memorandum was a set of forms designed to assist in assigning priorities and scheduling resources within the various projects concerned with the implementation of the information system.

2/ *Project Numbering System.* This was a standard system of numbering projects involved in the implementation of the information system.

3/ *Documentation System.* This described a standard method of documentation which was used in all projects concerned with the implementation of the information system.

4/ *Data Management System.* The data management system was a standard method of regulating data flow between the various operational units of the information system.

5/ *Standard Report Format.* This standard was designed to provide a uniform method of reporting information for use by groups involved in the implementation of the information system.

6/ *The Program Structure.* (This has already been described.)

7/ *Standard Measures of Programming Characteristics.* This involved standard measures of program content, program balance and regional involvement for use in the management reporting system, their formats and coding for data processing.

8/ *Standard Measures of Resources.* These standards involved measures of money, manpower, talent, real estate, equipment and purchased non-capital goods and services, their formats and coding for data processing.

9/ *Standard Measures of Effectiveness.* These measures were related to success in achieving objectives and were used in the management reporting system.

In addition to the above, the group established a data base committee, which considered all files and data sets that were candidates for admission into the common data base, using procedures similar to those described for establishing other standards.

Measures of Effectiveness and Use of Resources

The standards group approached the problem of establishing standard measures of effectiveness and use of resources by dividing these into three groups:

1/ Measures of effectiveness of the company in meeting prime objectives (Objectives 1, 2, and 3 in Table 10-1).

2/ Measures of programming characteristics, related to constraints applied by licensing regulations (Objectives 4, 5, 6, and 7 in Table 10-1).

3/ Measures of resources used by sub-units in the company in their work of progressing towards achieving objectives.

The approach was to produce a draft of a list of quantitative measures in each category, circulate this list for comment and discussion, produce a revised list embodying the concensus, and recirculate this revised list. By this means, over an elapsed time of twelve months, a first listing of acceptable quantitative measures was produced which was then used as a basis for a first version of the management reporting system. Some details of this first listing are given below.

Table 10-3
Measures of Effectiveness

Objective	*Quantitative Measure of Effectiveness*
Satisfactory return on investment	Percentage return on investment
Extension of radio and television services	Maximum potential radio and television audience size.
Programs with maximum popular appeal.	1. Achieved audience size by individual radio and television stations.
	2. "Appreciation Index" for individual programs (measuring audience reaction to these programs)

Measures of programming characteristics relating to objectives 4, 5, 6, and 7 of Table 10-1 are given in Table 10-4.

Table 10-4
Measures of Programming Characteristics

Measure	Purpose	Units	Classifications
1. Program Content	To measure program characteristics designed to achieve the objective of providing an expression of national identity.	% of hours of programming involving Canadian subject matter and employing Canadian talent.	by prφgram category, sub-category, prφgram element and sub-element by time of day.
2. Program Balance	To measure the balance of programming between information and entertainment for people of different ages, interests and tastes.	% of time in each prφgram element and sub-element.	by prφgram category, sub-category prφgram element and sub-element by audience grouping by time of day.
3. Regional Involvement	To measure program characteristics designed to achieve the exchange of cultural and regional information and entertainment, and the contribution of the company to the development of national unity and a national identity.	(a) amount and % of local programming (b) amount and % of network contributions from outside main centers (c) amount and % of exchange or programs between stations (d) amount and % of exchange of programs between stations of different languages.	by prφgram category, prφgram element and sub-element, by time of day.

The measures of resources initially accepted are shown in Table 10-5:

Table 10-5
Resource Measures

Resource	Units of Measure	Classifications
1. Money	Dollars	Budgetary Performance by pr∅gram category and element. Company Cash Flow.
2. Manpower	Man $\frac{\text{(years)}}{\text{(months)}}$ x Salary	by employee category by pr∅gram, sub-pr∅gram and activity.
3. Talent	Contracts x contact dollar value	by union affiliation by pr∅gram category and element.
4. Real Estate (a) Lands (b) Buildings	Area (sq. ft.) x $ value Area sq. ft. x imputed annual $ value (or monthly $ value)	owned or leased; by type or purpose; by pr∅gram category and element.
5. Equipment	Dollars, rent or depreciation	owned or leased; by type or purpose; by pr∅gram category and element
6. Purchased non-capital goods and services (including utilities and municipal taxes)	Dollars, purchased cost	by type; by pr∅gram categorv and element.

Data Processing Standards

The standards group commissioned a team of computer systems specialists (half from within the company and half contract personnel), to produce a listing of data processing standards as a preliminary to the work of redesign of computer supported systems. These standards were agreed between computer systems personnel in the company. Because of the technical nature of these standards, no managerial personnel took part in their formulation. The data processing standards established included:

- A data (file) management system for use throughout the company.

- Choice of clearly-specified versions of FORTRAN and COBOL as programming languages.

- Formats and coding for the quantitative measures established as standard and for associated descriptor material.

- Minimum standards for documentation of computer based systems and computer programs.

The choice of a data management system led directly to a choice of manufacturer for computer hardware. However, the decision was made at at this stage that the existing computer systems would remain until all new systems had been phased in and all new system development and initial operations should be conducted on commercial service-bureau facilities. The decision on whether to acquire hardware or to continue use of service-bureau facilities was thus deferred to a later time.

Once the initial data processing standards had been set, redesign of existing computer-based systems to operate under these standards was started.

Conduct of Seminars for Company Personnel

Soon after the start of Phase II of the implementation, the decision was made to hold a series of week-long seminars to explain the project to staff at all levels in the company. Some 300 personnel attended these sessions and all were advised to pass along the information gained to members of their own units. The schedule of one of these seminars is shown in Figure 10-2. Personnel attended in groups of 30 and the ten seminars were held over a four-month period. The majority of the sessions were given by members of the implementation team. Each seminar was opened by a senior vice-president and the president attended a dinner session during each week. These seminars were followed up by half-day presentations held at six-month intervals in the various parts of the company, in which progress and problems in the implementation were discussed.

Redesign of Completely Specified Systems

Existing computer-based systems were converted to operate under the agreed data processing standards according to a schedule of

Figure 10-2
Seminar Schedule

	SUNDAY	MONDAY	TUESDAY	WEDNESDAY	THURSDAY	FRIDAY
8:30		1. Company Management Philosophy (Senior Vice-President)	6. Techniques of Effective Management Responsibility and Authority	10. Information Systems – An Introduction	14. Management Science Techniques related to the Information System	16. Implementation Schedule in the Company
10:00		Coffee	Coffee	Coffee	Coffee	Coffee
10:30		2. Planning changes in Management Systems	7. Planning and Budgeting	11. Design of the Company Information System	14. Management Science Techniques (continued)	17. Seminar Evaluation and Discussion
12:00			LUNCH	LUNCH		
1:30		3. Human Aspects of Change	8. Planning and Budgeting (continued)	12. Computer Concepts related to the Information System	15. Panel Discussion	2:00 P.M. Depart
3:00		Coffee	Coffee	Coffee	Coffee	
3:30	5:00 P.M. Participants Arrive	4. Management by Objectives	Reading and Recreation	13. Problem solving and use of Computers	Reading and Recreation	
6:30			DINNER	DINNER	DINNER	
8:00	Seminar Opening	5. Discussion	9. After Dinner Speaker (President)	Computer Laboratory (Practical Use of Computers)	After Dinner Speaker (from a company that has already implemented an Information System)	

priority agreed by the committee of senior management. File-independence was incorporated into all new system designs. Master-files were created as the work proceeded and these were incorporated into the common data base through the administrative procedures of the data base committee. The first masterfiles were:

1/ Company personnel.

2/ Company staff positions.

3/ Suppliers of services to the company.

4/ Customers of the company.

5/ Broadcast programs.

6/ Artists used by the company.

7/ Capital assets.

After assimilating these relatively large masterfiles into the common data base, smaller data sets were added as the conversion proceeded. Compatible common data bases were established at the two divisional locations and arrangements were made for the three data bases to be brought up to date overnight, each with the other.

The following computer supported systems were converted in this first redesign:

1/ Payroll.

2/ General accounting and costing.

3/ Accounts receivable.

4/ Accounts payable.

5/ Broadcast scheduling.

6/ Inventory control.

Compatible components of these systems were installed at the two divisional locations.

The total effort involved in conversion to the new data processing standards, which included incorporation of interfaces and monitor routines in each system, was 114 man months over an elapsed time of about 12 months. The cost was $268,000.

The Management Reporting System – First Version

Early in Phase II, existing formal reports passing between the divisional responsibility centers and head office had been collected into a single document, without changing the format of these reports. As the development of standard quantitative measures of performance, programming characteristics and use of resources proceeded and as completely specified systems providing these data were converted, a new management reporting system format was designed. In the first instance, this related to reporting between divisional locations (Level 2) and head office (Level 1). The individual reports in this system are listed in Table 10-6. Examples of the format of these reports are given in Figures 10-3, 10-4, 10-5, and 10-6.

This new set of management reports was presented to management periodically along with the collection of existing reports and this procedure was maintained during a twelve-month period. At the end of this period, the new reports, which had been modified considerably as a result of comments by management, were adopted as the formal reporting system between Levels 2 and 1 in the company.

Summary of Phase II of the Implementation

The progress and development costs in Phase II of the implementation is shown in Figure 10-7. The development cost in this phase was $528,000, calculated as expenses on the project over and above normal operating costs of the company. At the peak of the work in this phase, 16 persons were engaged full time on the implementation, the greatest part of this effort being concerned with conversion of existing computer-based systems.

Table 10-6

Content of Initial Management Reporting System

Type of Report	Table Number	Report Title	Data Broken Down By
Company Financial Statements	Table 1	Company Balance Sheet	
	Table 2	Company Cash Flow	
Expenditure of Resources	Table 3	Operating Expenditures (see Figure 10-3)	English Radio, English TV
	Table 4	Revenue	French Radio, French TV (i.e., Program Category and sub-categories)
	Table 5	Capital Expenditures	as above
	Table 6	Use of Manpower (see Figure 10-4)	as above
	Table 7	Use of Manpower (monthly summary)	as above
	Table 8	Use of Artists	
Programming Characteristics	Table 9	National Content of Programs	English Radio, English TV, French Radio, French TV, Canadian, US and Foreign Programs, Prime-time and total-broadcast time
	Table 10	Program Balance (see Figure 10-5)	English Radio, English TV, French Radio, French TV, sub-elements of program element "Production"
	Table 11	Regional Involvement	English Radio, English TV, French Radio, French TV
Performance by Use	Table 12	Audience Size and Program Cost (see Figure 10-6)	Type of program (program sub-element)

Figure 10-3

Table 3

| Operating Expenditures ($000's) | | Months Ended | | | | |

Prøgram	Sub Prøgram	Months Ended 197		Current Fiscal Year Budget	Actual Expenditure for Corresponding Period in	
		Actual for Period	Budget for Period		Last Year	Year Before That
English Service	Radio					
	Television					
	Administration					
	Total					
French Service	Radio					
	Television					
	Administration					
	Total					
Corporate Management	Planning					
	Standards					
	Evaluation					
	Corporate Services					
	Head Office Local Services					
	Total					
Total All Prøgrams						

Figure 10-4

Table 6

Manpower Summary

For _____ Months Ended

Program	Sub Programs	Manpower Accumulated Costs – To Date		Establishment and Manpower Budget for Current Year		Accumulated Manpower Costs to Corresponding Monthly Period for Prior Years			
						Last Year		Year Before That	
		Average No. of Employees	($000's)	Number of Employees	($000's)	Average No. of Employees	($000's)	Average No. of Employees	($000's)
English service	Radio								
	Television								
	Administration								
	Total								
French service	Radio								
	Television								
	Administration								
	Total								
Corporate Management	Planning								
	Standards								
	Evaluation								
	Corporate Services								
	H.O. Local Services								
	Total								
Total All Programs									

Figure 10-5

Table 10

Broadcast Program Balance — Radio

Month of

English Service

	This Month %	One Month Ago %	Two Months Ago %	Twelve Months Ago %
Arts, Letters & Sciences				
Drama				
Feature Films				
Music				
News and Current Affairs				
Sports and Recreation				
Variety and Light Entertainment				
Total	100	100	100	100

French Service

	This Month %	One Month Ago %	Two Months Ago %	Twelve Months Ago %
Arts, Letters and Sciences				
Drama				
Feature Films				
Music				
News and Current Affairs				
Sports and Recreation				
Variety and Light Entertainment				
Total	100	100	100	100

Figure 10-6

Analysis of Programs Broadcast
English Television

Month	Year

Table 12

Activity Balance

Activity	Broadcast Time		Cost				Cost/Hour	Audience Size	Cost per 1000 Audience Hours
	Hours	%	Direct	Indirect	Total	%			
Arts, Letters and Sciences									
Drama									
Feature Films									
Music									
News and Current Affairs									
Sports and Recreation									
Variety and Light Entertainment									
Education									
Total All Activities									

Figure 10-7

Progress and Development Costs in Phase II of the Implementation

Start		Approximate Effort for Each Item*	
		Man Months	Cost ($)
12	Phase I	37	$88,000
14	Prøgram Structure Developed	12	$24,00
16	Establishment of Data Processing Standards	16	$28,000
17	Initial Ten-Seminar Schedule Completed	24	$134,000
22	First Up-Date Seminar Held	Small	Small
24	First Complete Listing of Quantitative Measures	20	$56,000
	First Version of Management Reporting System	8	$18,000
26	Conversion of Existing Computer-Supported Systems Complete	114	$268,000
	Total Phase II	194 Man Months	$528,000
Time (months)	Total Phase I and II	231 Man Months	$616,000

* The costs in these columns relate to full time effort in the implementation in excess of that provided for the normal operations of the company. They cover development effort by managers and information systems specialists that could be specifically related to the project. Where a staff member was seconded to the project for a significant time, his salary and other costs were includeded. Part-time work undertaken along with normal duties was not included.

Phase III of the Implementation

Having achieved a first version of the new information system in a 26-month period at a development cost of $616,000 (0.62% of annual revenues), the company senior management decided to consolidate the new system over the next two-year time period. Development costs during this period were to be limited to $100,000 per year and the full-time work force on new development was set at four persons. In effect, new development merged into normal operations during that period. Operating costs of data processing in the company dropped from the pre-implementation figure of $600,000 per year to $458,000 once conversion and acceptance of converted systems was complete. This was accomplished by virtue of the greater efficiency of the converted programs; and this reduction offset, to some extent, the development cost.

Achievements during the two year period of Phase III can be listed as follows:

- The new management reporting system was developed further and adopted as the formal company system between Level 2 and Level 1 36 months after the start of implementation.

- The management reporting system was extended to Level 3 in the company.

- Increased use was made of the historic store of data and an information retrieval system was introduced during this period.

- New computer-supported systems were introduced where these could be shown to be economic and operationally desirable.

Some General Comments on the Implementation

The case history in this chapter has been reported in the context of a single company, whereas the experience described was in fact drawn from three major implementations and several minor projects. In order not to detract from the flow of implementation detail, little mention has been made in the case history of difficulties encountered, of which there were many in each of the contributing projects. It is now proposed to go to the other extreme and report some of the major difficulties encountered, once again in the context of the Nationwide Broadcasting Company. As these problems are described, however, it will become clear that if all the difficulties described arose to a major extent in any one implementation, there would be little chance of success in that individual project. In the real-life projects, each of the difficulties occurred to a major or minor extent according to the conditions existing in each particular organization at the time of the implementation. It is in no way intended to imply that all the problems described here would arise in a major fashion in any one company.

Problems arising from the seeming imposition of a climate of greater rationality in decision making have already been described in general in Chapter 8. These problems caused continuing concern during the implementation at Nationwide. Only a proportion of the senior managers of the company were convinced at the outset of the value of the project being undertaken. Others, while not expressing opposition openly, did not give the project priority in their day-to-day direction of activities. Some resented the allocation of funds which they felt could have been put to better use, naturally, in support of their own activities.

Some senior managers, while actively supporting the project at first, became disheartened with the length of the project and the lack of tangible results in the first year. Others felt that their positions and status in the organization were being threatened. The opportunity to shine in a future crisis appeared to be lessening as the planning and evaluation horizons in the company were lengthened.

Younger managers, at lower levels, saw the opportunity to succeed and to appear more knowledgeable than their superiors by virtue of their greater formal education in management and use of computers. On the other hand, these younger staff members were constrained on some occasions from wholehearted support of the project by the knowledge that their future careers in the company depended in some measure on their present senior officers.

Difficulties were experienced in restraining information systems specialists from pressing the implementation when it was clear that the technical aspects of the work were advancing ahead of the appreciation of managers for these innovations. The effects of the necessary constraints on technical personnel sometimes resulted in frustration and a tendency to blame lack of progress on managers. Naturally, the information systems specialists regarded the implementation as the most important activity in the company. However, it was often necessary to postpone technical developments in order to ensure that they took their proper place with respect to the developing appreciation of the information system in the organization.

The introduction of a more formal planning and budgeting system linked to objectives and the emphasis given to evaluation of performance relative to goals caused concern at all levels of management. Senior managers felt that this method of management restricted their freedom to plan, and that their actions were to a large extent governed by conditions that could not be altered. This was in most cases caused by the managers taking too short a term view of planning. One manager complained, for example, that 70% of his budget related to personnel costs and that he could not reduce staff quickly. It was pointed out to him that even as low an annual figure of attrition as 5% would result in a substantial reduction in personnel costs over a five year period. If he allowed staff to decrease by this factor alone, he would soon have a correspondingly greater freedom of allocation of funds to other areas.

The distinction between the prøgram structure and the organization chart was misunderstood at all levels in Nationwide. The organization chart was found to be a major factor involved in estimates by staff members of their own and others' status in the company. Personnel concerned with status and job security regarded work on a prøgram structure as an indirect means of reorganization, and therefore as possibly threatening to their own position in the company.

There was opposition throughout the implementation from the financial branch of the company. Prior to the start of the project, data processing had been under the control of the finance department and had been almost completely devoted to producing financial reports. The effect of the implementation was to take data processing out of the control of the finance department and to reduce the volume of financial data by a considerable factor. This caused a number of clerical positions in the finance department to be declared redundant, which, in turn, was seen as a threat to the position of financial managers. In addition, these managers were asked to concentrate more on advising operating managers on financial *management* (an area in which they felt less qualified) and to undertake less financial *control* (an area in which they had been practicing for many years).

Opposition by the finance department took tangible shape in the acceptance phase of the conversion of computer-based accounting systems. In some cases, considerable delay was experienced in replacing existing systems which had been originally introduced by personnel in the finance department with converted systems introduced by the implementation team.

The importance attributed to standards in the implementation was interpreted by some managers as contributing to a loss of freedom of action. In some cases, only lip service was given to the establishment of standards, and these were not used extensively in some parts of the company until senior management insisted. Some managers maintained that "their" data was not the same as that used by other units of the company and could not therefore be part of a standard system. This resulted in some delays in establishing of the common data base.

The week-long seminars, perhaps inevitably, aroused expectations of quick changes in a project that was planned to extend over at least three years. Despite repeated statements to the opposite effect, some participants expected much more progress than was actually achieved. Follow-up sessions were ineffective in countering a degree of cynicism in those who expected quicker results, and who, in some cases, used this method of expressing overall opposition to the project.

Notwithstanding these difficulties, the implementation of an information system in the Nationwide Broadcasting Company was carried on throughout the three initial phases. The final judgment on benefits obtained from the system is not yet available. As with all such implementation projects, the work is continuing.

Index